Steve Lemco

253-826-6110 PST

stevelemco@aol.com

Reviews appreciated

Motorcycle Sales Made Easy

By

Steve Lemco

Copy Right

2012

Acknowledgements

Special thanks to following three awesome people for helping me with editing.

Roger Cooper – Corvallis, Oregon - For 40 years Roger has been the truest friend I have ever had. I am very proud that he calls me his friend. We were roommates when we were 23. I could write another book about those times. They were wild, crazy and so much fun. Most important of all is we were young and we did it right.

Judy Duthie – Sumner, Washington - Judy was my typing teacher in high school. If not for her I wouldn't have written one single word let alone 5 books. Every student should have at least one teacher they have a crush on and Judy was mine. She is still so pretty, full of life, and has a heart of gold. Judy is the most honorable love I have ever had. She will always be Miss Hendrickson to me.

Bill Hurley – Wilmington, Massachusetts – I do expect to hear great things in the future about this 18 year old. He has all the qualities it takes to reach the top. I feel qualified in spotting talent and I am sure that great things are in his future.

Table of Contents

Introduction

It is not my intent to say the same things the same way as I did in my first book You Gotta-Wanna. But I am going to be a little repetitious about the Bus Stop theory. I feel I really made some of my most valuable points pretty clear in that book. I honestly believe that if you buy into this theory you will not only become a better salesperson but you will also live a happier life. The two go hand in hand.

A lot of people including salespeople eternally are messed up with bad, sad and negative thoughts. It is not so much the problem that they are dealing with that is bringing them down. It is the negative thoughts that they are concentrating on that are bursting their bubble of contentment. I think it is impossible for you to be the best salesperson you can be if you are not at the top of your own personal game. Motivation and attitude are two of the most important ingredients to make anything work in sales or life. I'm sure everybody would agree with that.

I believe that you feel what you think. If you think about what you don't have, you will have nothing. If you think about what you do have, you will have everything. The beauty of all of this is that we have control over what we think.

I believe in the Bus Stop theory with all of my heart. I live by it and sell by it. I also believe in the Bus Stop concept for you and your life; but just as important, I believe in it for your customers. If you do too, then you will do all you can to help the customers enjoy the awesome pleasure of time spent riding their new motorcycle. You will try your best to uncover any objections they may have and do all you can to resolve them. I suggest that you don't do it for the one-time commission but do it for the years of pleasure your customers will experience.

Time is our most precious gift. It gives us the opportunity to do all the things that we have to do as well as the things we want to do. It is the gift that allows us to visit loved ones and friends, play with the kids and go on vacations. It is what allows you and your customers to ride your motorcycles and do so many wonderful things. Yes, time is our gold.

Consider what you would think if you only had an hour of time left. And most important of all is to realize that there is going to be a last hour in everyone's future including yours and mine. Once I got in tune with that idea I began taking more advantage of the days that I do have left. I began to waste less of them. I also became a much happier person and my sales increased dramatically.

Time is a limited quantity and it will run out. Once you have a firm grasp on that truth you will find that you really do not have the time to waste being deeply sad, mad or depressed. You can if you want. It is your life. The clock will still tick and the calendar will still flip. Time is bringing us all to the end of our time. So for me anyway, realizing that I am only temporary, and so much more temporary are my problems, I have become a very happy contented person. I then became a much better salesman.

Life is like a gas tank. If we are lucky at birth, we have a full tank; but it's the same as a disposable lighter. It is a one-time tank and it cannot be refilled. Look at the following line and place an X where you think your gas tank is at now. I placed mine there.

Full_____/_____Empty

I hope this helps you to not only realize how much fuel you have left in the game of life but to also understand that the miles behind you and the problems you once had are now a distant memory. What once upset you so much at one time means very little or nothing to you now. Won't this stand true in the future with anything that is bothering you at this time? Also remember the gas is always burning up.

You are always being brought into the future. As in the past, today's worries and problems will fade away with the days. The trick is to not feel the sadness, anger, and depressive thoughts now.

Again I will say that you will feel what you think. You are allowed to work on a problem to figure out a game plan to solve it without being sucked into it. You can whistle while you work. Everyone has this capability if they want to have it. But sadly some people are in their comfort zone when they feel bad. They have a bad self-induced condition called Stinking Thinking.

The simplicity to feeling good is: You Just Gotta-Wanna. Smokey the Bear might not have been right when he said, "Only you can prevent forest fires." In reality it was probably someone else's fault or maybe nature started the fire. But I know I am right when I say, "Only you can tell you what to think."

Once I looked at life this way I became a much better salesman. Most important of all I became a better person. I live each moment with appreciation. I see beauty everywhere. I look at those close to me with a smile in my heart. I also believe that now is the time to do the things I want to do as long as I can afford to do them.

This is where I am coming from. If a customer is dreaming about a new motorcycle and you make it affordable for them to get it, then "**NOW**" is the time to buy it.

A question you should ask all of your customers after they have picked out their desired model is, "Would you be happier if you had one?"

Of course they are going to say yes. If you understand what I am saying, you will then realize that you are not trying to sell someone something that they don't want just so you will get paid. Instead you are helping someone to have a happier life by enjoying something that they have probably wanted for years. Something they will enjoy for many years to come. And yes, you still get paid, and everyone wins.

You can buy a lot of things with money but nobody can buy back yesterday. If a new motorcycle would make the customer have a better life, then you owe it to them to do your best to help them to buy it now. If they do, you have also helped them to have a better time in life by living the dream. Now their yesterdays will be filled with the awesome memories of riding.

Many customers who did not buy were never shown how easy and affordable you can make it to own. I will be talking a lot about that subject in the chapter: How Much Is It.

Chapter One
The Bus Stop

The Bus Stop Theory is Just AN ATTITUDE. You think you go to work, come home, watch television, eat, sleep, play, go shopping, and do a thousand other odds and ends throughout the day. You think that's what's happening, and indeed it is. But while all that is going on so is your life.

For the most part life is about occupying time. Time is the most precious thing that we possess. Without it there is not much more to think about. It is worth more than a fortune but yet so many people spend it unwisely. Not so much in the things that they do but by how they are feeling internally while doing them.

I don't think it's much of a secret that all of us were born and all of us will die. Saying it like that sounds a bit morbid and makes it difficult to talk about.

I like to say that when you are born the Bus drops you off then comes back to pick you up at the end of your time. Every birthday means you were lucky enough to spend another year at the Bus Stop. We are all just occupying time at the Bus Stop while we are waiting for the Bus to pick us back up. If you think about it, I am sure you will agree that the best you can do at the Bus Stop is to say that you enjoyed the wait.

I'm at my 59th year at the Bus Stop. One thing that I know for certain is that I didn't get picked up during my first 58 years of life. I don't know if I'll be catching the bus this year – I won't know that until my 60th birthday rolls around.

I figure at best, if I stay lucky, I have twenty-four good years left. Twenty-four years sounds like a lot. Plenty of time to do the things that matter most. But consider this. I sleep and average of eight hours a night, so in the next twenty-four years I'll sleep away one third of them.

That leaves only sixteen years of wakefulness before I'm twenty-four years older.

And, of course, from the time I get up to go to work in the morning until I get back home at night I've spent half of my awake time dealing with work. That's eight years. So let's see, I might have twenty-four good years waiting at the Bus Stop, less eight sleeping, less eight working. That leaves only eight years to live my life, doing things that really count like riding my motorcycle.

I've still got to shower and shave, take the kids here and there, mow the lawn, take out the garbage, fix the car, and so on. I calculate I'll spend half of my non-sleeping, non-working time doing things I wish I didn't have to do but they needed to get done. There goes another four years, leaving me just FOUR years to do what I really like to do while I'm at the Bust Stop. I don't know about you, but with only four years of the really good time left, I don't want to waste any of it waiting for the Bus with a bad attitude.

Think about that. Maybe we don't have as much time left as we thought we did and neither do your customers. If a motorcycle will help then have a better time at the Bus Stop then we should do our best to help them buy one as soon as possible.

Believe me, if they do buy, they will be a lot happier than you. I will always believe that the winner is the buyer. I sincerely believe we don't sell motorcycles; what we do is help people to have a more enjoyable Bus Stop.

The Bus is still going to pick me back up if I have a good or bad attitude. The Bus driver will still have me hop on board if I am rich or poor, happy or sad. When the time comes to get back on the Bus, that's all there is to it. Just ask Elvis, John Wayne, or Michael Jackson. It doesn't matter who you are or where you are. When the Bus Driver stops, everyone climbs on board.

When your Bus shows up, how will you wish you spent your time waiting for it? Being happy or sad, motivated or depressed, it has always been your choice. It's your choice now.

Where am I going with this? Does the attitude you choose in your personal life have anything to do with being a top salesman? I believe it has everything to do with it.

How do I know? Consider this: When you're working, you're also spending time at the Bus Stop. I don't believe you can have a bad attitude about life and then show up at work and turn on a switch for the positive energy it takes to be a top salesperson. I'm sure that you already know it takes good positive energy to reach your potential.

Attitude has everything to do with ultimate success–the best part is that it's all within your control. It always has been. There is no charge for feeling great but there is a self-inflicting charge for feeling like crap.

I hope to spend a long time at the Bus Stop and I bet you do too. However along the way, wives and husbands can leave us, death and destruction can cross our paths, thieves can break in and steal everything we've spent a lifetime acquiring.

But who can take your honor away from you? Who can steal your heart? Who can take your attitude away from you? No one can but you. You can give them away, but they can never be stolen. Honor, heart, and attitude don't cost a dollar, yet are a very valuable part of your life.

Dog Poop

Have you ever stepped in dog poop? It's a bummer. Especially when you don't discover it until you're in your car. I hate it when that happens. Bummer!

Bummer is a good word to describe something you wish didn't happen, but you know what...it did happen... Bummer... I sometimes believe that dogs were created so they would leave piles in our yard so we'll step in them and learn how to handle the other problems we have in our lives.

Now if your head caught on fire I would not expect you to say, "Bummer, my heads on fire." I am sure you would be a bit more animated than that. But most of life's bummers are not that drastic and are easy to wipe off.

Let me explain. It's a beautiful day and everything is wonderful, when splat – you step in the big one. AHHHH, BUMMER! You moan, you groan, then what? You wipe it off, of course. Finally you clean your shoe off. Now what? Yep, it's full steam ahead continuing to have a good day; it was just a minor setback.

If you don't want to step in it again, walk with your head down and your eyes trained on the ground. You'll look pretty weird and you won't get anywhere fast but you also won't step in anything unpleasant.

But that's not what you do, is it? You moan and groan a bit after discovering what you've just stepped in but then you just wipe it off and keep on walking-going full steam ahead. You don't spend a long time dwelling on what you've just wiped off. You aren't going to cancel the rest of the day and call everyone you know to tell them what you just stepped in, are you?

We've all been taught how to handle *other people's* problems very well. Have you ever been out walking around with a good friend, and then splat they step in it. You're probably laughing your butt off (discreetly if you don't want to get slugged.) What's your friend doing? He's muttering, "Why me" Bummer.

If you understand what I'm saying, why didn't we laugh the first time it happened to us? It's because we took it personally. We sometimes let these things reach into our soul. It's OK to say bummer at the time a problem arises but the sooner you wipe it off the sooner you will feel better. Yes, we might have to deal with an unpleasant situation; but like I said earlier, you can whistle while you work.

I have often witnessed salespeople lose their pizazz because a deal got turned down, a customer changed their mind, or a be-backer didn't be-back. Because of this they often miss a sale because of their down attitude. Or two sales or three...They made it more than a bummer and became their own worst enemy instead of their own best friend. You know, the kind of best friend who cheers you up when bummers happen. You do have the power to do that. Everyone does.

It doesn't have to happen this way but sometimes it does. Sometimes bad things happen to good people; it's just the way life is. We cannot always control circumstances, but at all times we can control our attitude about those circumstances.

Do you remember when you were a little kid and mom turned off your cartoon? You threw yourself on the floor and cried. You felt like it was the end of your world. You knew you would never be happy again. At that time in your life, if you were in absolute control, you would have commanded that every channel show cartoons twenty-four hours a day. Mom had no way to convince you that it was just a cartoon and not all that important. There would also be no way to convince you that one day you would watch the news instead of a cartoon.

Then you became a little older and wiser and cartoons didn't mean as much to you. But what if your G.I. Joe or your Barbie doll broke or got lost then *there goes the attitude!*

As time passes you grow up and discover that your toys are no longer important to you. Then one day you meet your first true love and you're in heaven. But if he or she finds another person to love instead of you, well, you end up with a broken heart. You think that you will never love again.

How long and how many unpleasant situations do we experience before we figure out this little poem I wrote:

TIME COMES,
THINGS CHANGE.
OUR PROBLEMS WILL FADE
AWAY WITH THE DAYS
SO FEEL GOOD NOW

Isn't the past a great place to have a problem? I don't mind one bit – now – the problems I used to have. But what was it like when I was going through one of those big problems? I'm talking about grown-up choices to make: (1) Moan and groan and cry and lie there in a state of depression, then, finally take care of the problem.

Or (2) moan and groan some, wipe it off by taking care of the problem and then move on. Either way, whatever it was that I thought was such a problem will soon enough seem like a cartoon that I didn't get to finish. I know that it will seem that way when I am getting back on the Bus so I elect to do it much sooner. I have too many good things to appreciate. There is not enough time to waste on being negative.

THEY SAY YOU CAN'T take your money with you. They should say you can't take your problems with you. Go to a cemetery sometime, wait until no one alive is within earshot then shout out, "Hey! Does anyone have a problem?" Nope, you won't hear anybody talking about how a car won't start or rent is way overdue.

If it was your resting place and I was talking to you, I am sure you wouldn't care even if I told you that your worst enemy was out riding your motorcycle. (Hard to believe isn't it?) Even if your spouse was on the back of it, you still would not complain.

Nope, nobody will complain. I believe that the people buried underground are now certain of what I am talking about. They have come to understand that all their troubles, worries, heartache and disappointments are just cartoons that they didn't get to finish. The trick is to know this while you are above ground.

Everything we accomplish, everything we have, good or bad, is temporary. We rent or we lease. There is no option to buy. We're just waiting at the Bus Stop. When the Bus comes back for us, we aren't allowed to take any of our possessions–or our problems – with us. To me, the secret to life is making the most of my time while waiting for the Bus. I hope to do the best I can without hurting others. I hope to help a few people along the way, just as others have helped me.

HAVE YOU EVER NOTICED that when you have a problem and you become stressed and depressed over it, you now have three problems?

Your tire goes flat. Instead of moaning and groaning a little and saying "Bummer!" then fixing the tire, you elect to let it reach into your soul. You smack the trunk as you open it, only to discover that your spare tire is flat too. Now you go crazy. You kick the side of the car, pound on the hood. You end up having to walk home. (By the way, have you noticed that, for people with stressed attitudes, the spare always seems to be flat?)

When you finally arrive home on foot, your spouse wants to know where the car is and why you're limping and what happened to your hand? You're not in the mood to go into details, so you get grumpy and take it out on him or her. Well, it's not very likely that they will become understanding at that moment, not with *your* attitude, so the spouse pops off at you. There goes the nice, relaxing dinner. The only thing left to do is bring the kids down so you yell at them. Now they're upset with you, too, and rightfully so.

Heck, let's complete the day. As you remember what you stepped in a couple of days ago you notice the dog is sitting in front of you wagging his tail, looking at you with loving eyes. Wham! He goes flying across the room off the end of your foot.

By the next morning, after sleeping on the couch, you've mellowed out. You apologize to your spouse, take the family out for lunch, tell the kids you're sorry, and pick them up a gift. You take the dog to the vet and pay the bill.

Okay. You've done your best to get things back to normal you hope. Naturally, you had to do all this in your spouse's car because – oh, yeah – you still need to fix the tire. You better get to it before you start making *more* problems. And, if you're smart, you'll fix the spare while you're at it.

Do you see where I'm going? We can't do much about tires going flat or any of the other dog pile things that happen, but we can do everything about how we handle them. Do you honestly believe that in six years and two months you will remember changing that tire? Sure, it was a bummer at the time–but even if you do remember, you certainly won't care. You had lived all your life until then not thinking about that tire. After you fix it, you won't give it another thought until it happens again. Then what? Chances are you will handle it in the same way you did the last time.

Think of the problems you've experienced in the past; how did you handle them? Have you let one problem cause others? If you have, turn it into a good thing: You are now in a position to learn from your mistakes. Of course, learning is one thing and applying what we've learned is another. If you do both, you will have a much better time at the Bus Stop.

YOU ARE ASKING THE QUESTION, What does all this have to do with sales? That's a good question. I, however, have a question for you: Which salesperson do you think sold more units today? The one who moaned and groaned and fixed the tire? Or the one who alienated their spouse, yelled at the kids, and kicked the dog?

Selling is, and always will be, a game of numbers. Many times you will do your best and still end up without a sale. It works that way in life. If we allow our moods to be dictated by the results of our efforts, our attitude is ruled by what we don't control. The hand that bounces the rubber ball is no longer yours. But if you and your efforts bounce back up after each letdown, you will end up with many more positive results. It's all in the hand that bounces the ball. Nobody can control the ball one hundred percent of the time. But our efforts and attitudes are one hundred percent controllable. A good attitude is yours for free (so is a bad one).

A good attitude is a key secret to sales and life. It's not much of a secret – it's there inside of us all, just waiting to be called upon.

Chapter Two
What Makes a Great Salesperson

While flying home to Seattle after a sales hiring and training job in New York, I was talking to the man sitting next to me. I told him what I did for a living. He had a simple question that required me to think deep about the answer. He asked me what makes a great salesperson.

I thought about it and reflected back to all the salespeople and sales managers I have trained over the past forty years. I have met some amazing great salespeople all across the US as well as England, France, Wales, New Zealand and Australia. Yes, I have met many top salespeople.

My first reply to my fellow passenger was in order to be a top salesperson you should be genuine, true, honest, and sincere. You should have a burning desire to help the customer live the dream by helping them buy the motorcycle they have been dreaming about. But these qualities will not come together if they are made up and don't come from the heart. You can only put on an act for a short while before your true nature is revealed.

I have coached many salespeople who could put on an act but fell short when it came to getting the sale because the customer felt like the salesperson was not sincere and they were only trying to get the sale. They were only thinking of themselves and not caring about the customer's needs. Nobody likes to be sold. People want to feel like they bought the motorcycle and I am sure you would too.

There are three concepts that a top salesperson must believe. The first one is: *The winner is the buyer not the seller*. You will sell a ton of bikes over the years and the dealership needs to move several bikes a day so the one bike you just sold did not change the lives of you or the owner of the dealership. But my friends, you have greatly changed the life of the customer. You did a very good thing. Life is short, riding time is even shorter. You have taken a dreamer and fulfilled his dream.

The second concept is: You do not sell a bike; you help people buy them. If you will be true and have a strong desire to help someone have a better life then you will find that you get many more sales. Also the customer who believes you are their friend, because you are, will be a loyal repeat customer for life and many times send in friends and relatives to buy a motorcycle from you.

Concept number three is: You must believe that people do not shop for what they do not want. Yes, most customers say that they are just looking. But what they are looking for is a trustworthy salesperson that is also just looking. The salesperson is just looking to make their customer's dream come true.

So what makes a good salesperson? Basically be good person. One who is honest and speaks truthful words. Now if they speak true words with a Gotta-Wanna attitude, good things have to happen. The beauty to all of this is that everyone has control over being a good person.

We all know what a good person is and if you have fallen short on this attribute you have also fell short in sales. It has to work that way and the best part is: if you know you need to make some changes with your life, then you are 100% in control to make those changes. You Just Gotta-Wanna.

If you control the things that are controllable and it shows in your walk and talk, people will take to you. They will trust you because you are trustworthy. But of course there is a lot more to do with your customers besides being a person who cares about them.

You must be able to hold informative and interesting conversations. The relationship you develop with your customers has more to do with the sale than anything else. I believe that most customers will buy from someone they like and trust even if they can save a little money at another dealership where they don't care for the salesperson.

You must know your product. If you don't know some of the basic often-asked questions, you will come across like a salesman only interested in a commission. They have the right to ask the questions and they also deserve to get the answer. When you can answer their questions the customers will be impressed and believe in you that you love your product.

I don't want to belittle anything about sales, but four things are of the upmost importance. I will go into detail about them in future chapters.

You must make a friend out of the customers by listening to their wants, desires and dreams. Asking the right questions is the surest way of doing that.

You must know how to make the price affordable. Once the money is affordable a sale is almost always going to follow.

You must….I repeat… you must ask everyone to buy today. You must ask them more than once. It is not that you always come right out and ask if they want to buy it. But you guide them to the question by offering options and ways they can buy today.

You must love using the telephone. It works two ways. You get incoming calls that many time lead to sales. But you also should stay in touch with your customers through follow-up calls. It should never be one and done. Sometimes it may take as many as ten calls to close the deal. Many times it is about planting small seeds of the customers owning the motorcycle they are dreaming about. Then one day they wake up from the dream and make it reality. It will be only natural that they think of you at purchase time because you were their friend and you stayed in touch with them.

The beauty of sales is anyone can be a pro at it. Anyone can be a great salesperson. The key ingredients are your personality, mixed with knowledge, truth, sincerity and a true Gotta-Wanna desire to have your customers out riding the bike of their dreams instead of dreaming about it. You are not really a salesperson but a dream fulfiller. You are the Santa Claus of sales.

You Gotta Believe In Order To Receive

I have been doing sales training / hiring for the past 40 years. Several times while flying to my destination I am asked what I do for a living. I think about it and then say, "Nothing. I tell other people what to do and they're supposed to do it. I then smile to myself and recall the many sales journeys I have had over the past 40 years.

"How did you get good enough to be an instructor," I am frequently asked.

I tell them three things.

I don't lie

I don't scam

I don't keep secrets.

Number one and two are pretty self-explanatory and I mean it 100% of the time. I don't lie and I have never scammed to get a sale. Number three is probably the biggest secret of all to have a successful sales career.

First, you must believe that you are selling a great product. You must believe that you work for a first-class dealership and that they will stand behind the product. You must sincerely desire to help the customer buy from you today. That's all great, but it will do you no good if you keep it a secret. You must show your true nature of desiring to help someone be happy. You must tell them all the good things you know about the motorcycle and dealership. They cannot read your mind.

Every dealership for the most part has the same bike, same color and same price. What we need to have is a stronger desire to get the business today than our competition. There are two ways we let our customers know this. We show them in our demeanor and tell them simply with words.

No customer should ever leave the dealership who did not hear more than once that we would love to earn their business today. They should be shown your operation with pride because it is built on pride. Whatever you do, don't keep these things a secret.

There are some secrets we need to get reveled. Like, what bike is the customer interested in? Do they have one now? Are they married? If so does the spouse ride? Do they plan on going on any long trips? So on and so forth. It's called talk Ping-Pong. If you ask the question (Ping) they will answer. (Pong.) Back and forth you will go as long as you wish to carry on the conversation.

Again, the customer knows he can get the same model elsewhere. The number one thing that convinces them to buy from you... is... You. The fact that you shared your beliefs and desires to obtain their business and you listened to their wants and dreams. By playing a good game of talk Ping-Pong you will obtain your fair share of sales today and increase the number of future sales.

Sales should be fun. It always has been for me. I do my best to make it fun to hear what I have to say to a customer on the floor or to a student in my seminar. It is very important to believe in these things. When training others I always share my rhyme: Believe and receive. Doubt and you're out.

You Only Have To Be Good One Day – Today.

The key aspect to sales and life is to be self-motivated to do the best you can. Nobody can stop you from trying your best. You own your efforts outright. You are the captain of what thoughts you allow yourself to think about and what actions you will take.

Everyone I know wants to have good results. Every salesman wants their customer to purchase from them. But that is not your decision. Yes, you can greatly influence the customers but ultimately the decision to purchase is theirs.

What you can control 100% of the time is your attitude and efforts. There are two things I want to say about these two subjects.

Attitude – Once again I will say this: You will feel what you think. If you think and focus about sad things like a deal that got turned down, you will feel sad. If you think of funny things, you will laugh. If you think of motivational things, you will be motivated. The best part is: Nobody but nobody can tell you what to think. Learn from your mistakes and learn from your successes. If you do those two things, you will have a lot to motivate yourself.

Good results are the children of motivated efforts. I feel this is worth saying again. *Good results are the children of motivated efforts.* Again, who can stop you from trying your best? Only you.

Many people are their own worst enemy. They stand in the way of their own success. If you are your own best friend and motivate yourself to give your best effort, I don't see how you can fail. No, you won't win every time. You won't get a hit every time you come to bat, and you won't get every sale. But you will make the salesman All-Star team and I like your chances of moving up. It's really not that hard. You only have to control that which you can control. If you do that I believe good things will happen to you.

When I do sales training I teach a seven step system.

1 – Greet
2 – Probe
3 – Sit on the bike
4 – Presentation / Demonstration
5 – Sit at desk

---

6 – Write-Up
7 – Close and maybe close again and again

Notice that I drew a couple of lines after step 5. That's because the first five steps you control. Nobody will stop you from saying hi. They will be more than happy to tell you about themselves and what they are interested in. If you offer, they are almost always willing to sit on the motorcycle they have been dreaming about. Of course they want to hear what you have to say and probably would love a demonstration if they qualify for one. And yes, if you built a good relationship with them they will be more than happy to sit at your desk even if it is to get a card and have you thank them for their time.

Once you have learned how to be a good showman today all you have to do is repeat what you already know. It's like the movie *Ground Hog Day.* Life and sales can be very repetitive. We should become great at the things we do on a daily basis. Study yourself, look for your weaknesses and strive to strengthen them. Look at your strengths; use them to help you work on your weaknesses and also remember them during times of bummers.

Chapter Three
Greeting the Just Lookers

Before I start talking about different fun ways to greet your customers I have a question for you. Have you ever wondered why the customers are there? Sure, they are interested in the idea of owning a new motorcycle. Either that or they are out shopping for something they don't want. If you think about that then it should make no sense to you that someone would take the time to do that. So of course they are interested in your product.

It is very important to believe that the customers really want what you have to offer. It is very important for the customers to believe that you really want to help them to be happier. If you mix those two things together along with a Gotta-Wanna attitude and desire, good things are bound to happen.

In this day and age a lot people do extensive research on the computer. It is not uncommon that some customers know more about the motorcycle then the salesperson does. Yet, when they walk in they still say, "I'm just looking."

Yes, it is quite a bit more impressive to see and touch the actual motorcycle than it is to see a picture or video on it. So when the customer is in your dealership, it is truly a huge time of advantage. It is an advantage to the customer because he has an awesome salesperson who will eventually ask the question, "Would you be happier if you had one?"

I would bet at least 95% of the customers will say yes to that question. So it is another huge plus for the customer because they are talking to a salesperson who wants to make them happy.

When they do say yes to that question you should follow up by saying, "Great. I would love to make you happy." Do you know why you should say that? Hopefully it's because you really do want to make them happy and you are not keeping it a secret.

I know there are times when customers come in to buy on the spot. They are the easy deals. You would have to hit on their wives or call their kids ugly in order for them not to buy. But we know that in the real world most customers say, "Just looking" right after you greet them.

So why are the customers there? Why do they say they are just looking? I believe that they are just looking for a salesperson to be honest and sincere and have a true desire to overcome any objections that might come up. Always knowing that the customers do want a new or pre-owned motorcycle.... really bad.... really, really bad. I feel that you must believe that and want them to have it really bad too.

You must know going in that it is not so much the motorcycle that needs to be sold but rather your being prepared to find out and overcome objections. This is the most important mission.

Many times the customer's objection was never found out from the salesperson. That salesperson is left with the mystery of: *Why someone did not buy what they wanted?* If only the salesperson did find out what was holding the customer back from buying then they might have overcome the objection. Sometimes it's as simple as asking, "What's stopping you from buying today? Maybe we can help figure it out."

The saddest part about a lost sale is that the customer is still a dreamer instead of living the dream. Remember you are a dream- come-true-maker. Always believe that the winner is the buyer. I will offer some advice later in the chapter: *Finding the true objection* but for now let's stick with the greetings.

I am not so concerned about what you say when you greet someone as it's pretty basic, logical and common sense. Things like, "Good morning. Thanks for coming in. Hi, how are you? Welcome to Steve Motors," and so on.

It's not so much what you say when you greet someone as it is how you said it. Again it is too basic to go on and on about having a cheerful mannerism and a smile. I am more concerned that you are prepared for the customer's reply to your greeting.

One of my favorite things to hear a customer say is, "I'm Just Looking." It would be crazy not to love hearing it and not being prepared for it because it will be the opening comment by 95% of all customers.

I made it easy for me to love because I finish the statement in my head to get my attitude on right. When they say, "Just Looking," I continue by thinking, "They are just looking to buy a motorcycle right now from me." I will say it again. They are just looking to buy a motorcycle right now from me! Wow! Cool! You must always believe that. Why not? Which way do you think is a better way to come to bat? Afraid of the pitcher and holding back or confident you can get a hit. Mind-set is extremely important to sales as it is in many other things in life.

If a customer said they were just looking to buy right now to a salesperson, the salesperson would smile and say something like, "Super, glad to hear it." So say that anyway. Congratulate the customer for being in the looking stage. None of us have ever sold anything for the most part if the customer was not interested in what we had to offer. What they are really just looking for is a salesperson that will make it easy to buy.

Take a look at the word GREET

The *G* stands for Glad.

When a customer hears the greeting they should have no doubt by the body language and smile that the salesperson is Glad to see them. If the salesperson is not, then they should go home. The last thing we want is a customer that is Glad to be looking at their dream bike talking to a salesperson who would rather be doing something else.

The *R* stands for Ready.

Are you Ready to go? Are you Ready to hear, "Just Looking?" Are you Ready to open your customer up and have them tell you all the reasons why this bike will make them happier?" Are you Ready to lead them to the bike and then to your desk to get a write-up? Are you Ready for the entire procedure?

The first _E_ is for Enthused

Are you Enthused about helping someone have a better time in life by enjoying a new or pre-owned motorcycle? Are you Enthused that you can change someone's life for the better? Are you Enthused that the best person that they can buy it from is you because you care as much after the sale as you do making it.

The second _E_ is for Eager

Are you Eager to listen to the customer's wants, desires and stories? Are you Eager to tell them what a first-class dealership you represent and also show them around while introducing them to some of the other employees that work with you? Are you Eager to fulfill their dream?

The _T_ stands for Tuned In to all of the above.

If you are Tuned in then you will never greet a customer by saying, "Can I help you?" That is how strangers are greeted. Our customers are our friends and you would not say to a friend, "Can I help you?"

There are many good greetings like the simple, "Hi. How are you?" Or, "Welcome, so glad you came by today." We have lots to look at. Are you looking for new, used, sport bike, touring or anything in particular?"

By the time you have given these options you have moved to the probing stage. A super greeting only takes seconds but those seconds can set up the sale, as much for the salesperson as it is for the customer.

27

All professional baseball players go on deck before they go to bat. They get mentally prepared for something they have been doing since they were a kid. If the best players in the world do that then I hope you do too. You should always be mentally prepared and in tune with the selling process.

There are many things that take place as you get prepared to greet a customer. The most important one of all is that you are in the greeting mode. You are Glad, Ready, Enthused, Eager and Tuned In.

Chapter Four
The Art of Probing
&
S.O.B.

The Probe - is a never ending step. It is also the heartbeat of the sale. Probing is the ability to make a friend out of a complete stranger in a short amount of time. Proper probing is the surest way to develop a good relationship between you and the customers.

You will never ask the customer to go back outside so you can greet them again. Chances are once they sit on the bike they will not sit on it again. Such is true with all of the steps. But the probe begins from the moment you talk to the customer for the first time and doesn't end until you never speak to them again.

My definition of the Probe will not be found in the dictionary but it should be. Again, my definition of the Probe is: *The ability to make a complete stranger a friend in a short amount of time.* If they don't buy today then we most certainly want to be their friend in the motorcycle business and follow up for future sales.

Probing is something you can always practice. Every time you go through a checkout stand you can practice being friendly and start a short conversation while they are ringing up your purchase. Introduce yourself and get their name and tell them two things.

Tell them you think they are doing a terrific job. (Unless there not. I will never ask you to lie.) But if you think they are doing a good job then don't keep it a secret.

Let them know what you do for a living. If they or someone they know is interested in a new motorcycle, offer them a business card or two.

We run into people we don't know all the time. Take a second or two to say hello with a smile. Sometimes you might try to start a short conversation. You will be amazed how many sales this will make you.

Yes, it may only make you a few sales a year from the people you meet by chance. Many of them will not be interested in motorcycles and don't want to be riders. But it will help you to stay in shape being a good Prober and help make many sales from the customers who walk into your dealership who are obviously interested in your product.

After you greet them you can always count on the customer saying, "Just looking," "Great, we have a lot to look at." would be a super answer followed up by some choices. I will get to the choices soon but do you know why you say something like, "Great, glad to hear it?" It's because it is great. You are glad to hear it. Don't keep it a secret. Where would you be if the customer was not looking? Don't keep your pleasure of helping them a secret. They can see it in your demeanor and hear it in your greeting.

"Great, are you looking for new, used, sport bike, touring, anything in particular?"

You should never follow a "Just Looking" reply with something like, "Anything in particular." This is an essay question that requires the customer to be defensive and you are forcing him to answer. Right away you are putting them in an uncomfortable position.

By giving them multiple choices they only have to pick one. You are now in control and you are making it easy to begin a good relationship that can turn into many sales over time. Not just with them, but also with their family and friends. It is OK to say anything in particular as long as you gave them other model options before or after you said it.

Once you have greeted the customer with a cheerful smile in a friendly mannerism, you are in a position to develop a friendship and remove the skepticism that many customers have toward salespeople.

The best way to make a friend out of a complete stranger is to listen to what they have to say. This is done by asking questions about

30

the customer's interests be it about their life or the motorcycle they are seeking. Make sure you are focused on their answers and look for the comments that will be easy to get them to continue talking. Everyone loves to be listened to and that is what friends do.

One great question to ask the customer is: "What got them interested in their choice model?" Most of the time you will get one of two answers, either they will say that someone they know has one or they have been reading about it. A perfect follow up to that statement is, "What did your friend or article say about it." Rest assured they will say good things or they would not be in your dealership looking at it. This will at times convert your customer to becoming their own salesman. It is much better to have the customer tell you how great the bike is than you.

A question I feel is of the upmost of importance is, "Would you be happier if you had one? If they say no, then you have my permission to say, "Please don't buy one." But really, who would say no to that question?

Once you have heard them say they would enjoy life more with a new motorcycle then you should not be a salesman trying to make a commission but a 'Help you to be a Happy-Man' trying to make your new friend happy.

You might ask the following questions while you and the customer are looking at the bike. Maybe when they are sitting on it or maybe while they are at your desk. Just be sure to ask questions that will put them in tune with their desires. The customer is chalk full of information for the asking.

Do you have a motorcycle now?

Have they ever had a motorcycle?
If so, what do they have or had and what is their favorite story about it.

Are they married? If so does their spouse ride?

Will they be riding it to work? Where do they work?

Will they be taking any long trips on it? If so, where are they going and when do they plan on leaving?

Will they be going with any of their friends? If so, who are they? What do they ride?

Do they have any children? Do they have a picture of them?

These are just a few of the probing questions you should ask. I am sure you can think of many more. Getting your customer to talk about themselves and their desires is the surest way to make a friend out of a complete stranger. Sure we want the sale but at the least the customer should feel they made a friend in the business and when the time is right for them to buy they will think of you.

I could go on and on about the importance of making a friend in the business with every customer, but I am sure you know that. Yes, you should talk about the bike, things like features and benefits. But I am pretty sure nobody ever called up their friends or their mother to tell them about how great someone was because they knew everything about the bike.

They will tell their friends and mom that the salesperson they talked to was really cool and spent time getting to know them and their wants, desires and interests. Hey, they even took time out to look at pictures of their children.

When I am doing sales seminars, I would say that I spend an hour or more just on that last paragraph. It is what selling is all about. Of course we would like everyone to buy from us today, but that is never going to happen. But what can always happen is applying our efforts to get involved in a common ground conversation to reassure the customer that there is more to us then just being a salesperson trying to get their hard earned money. It really works great when it's the truth. Just don't keep it a secret.

If you had a friend in the car business, and you were looking for a car, where would you go to buy one? I bet you would go and see your friend.

The customer will have several options of where to purchase the motorcycle but there is only one place where you are. If you become your customer's friend in the business you will get more bikes bought from you that day and double your future sales especially if you do follow-up calls.

If you and the customer got to talking about baseball, football, golf, racing, movies, music and the list goes on and on, then you have made a friend. If you can't get the sale today then you have greatly increased your chances of getting it later. Also by discussing such things you will find it greatly benefits you when you do a follow up call. Now you have many subjects to discuss with them besides just the motorcycle.

One of many things I always suggest at my seminars is to watch the news, sports and weather every night so you are caught up on current events giving you many things to talk about with your customer.

Actually if you are probing the right way, you would mention a topic and if the customer was interested in it, let them tell you all about it and how they feel. You will learn many important and helpful things about someone if you keep them talking about their points of view.

Remember, the probing stage never ends. It is ongoing throughout the entire process. The best talker is also the best listener. How do you listen? Just put a what, where, how, which, when or why in front of a comment made by your customer. If you do, it will not be long before they think of you as their friend rather than the salesperson.

S. O B.

S. O. B. Stands For: 'Sit – On - Bike.' It is a very
important step. Not just for obvious reasons such as the customer getting to feel the thunder underneath them, but it is also about you being in control.

For the most part customers will not say "No, please don't greet me." Neither will they stop you from being friendly and building a good relationship. But they might say, "No, that's ok, I don't want to sit on it. I'm afraid I might buy it."

Taking sales one step at a time is the key. Salespeople need to trust that if they hear a customer say no… it does not always mean no. If a customer said no to the comment from a salesperson of, "Here go ahead and have a seat on it and see how she fits." Then it is time to guide the customer so we can follow the steps.

The best way I know of changing the customer's mind is to slap the seat and say something like, "Awe go ahead; it's Ok. Have a seat and check it out."

Many a time all that the customer needed was reassurance that it was OK to straddle the bike of their dreams. If I had built a fun relationship with the customer, I used to take the mirrors and turn them a bit so the customer would see themselves. I would then say, "That's what everyone else will be seeing." Normally we would both chuckle. Do you know why I would say that? It's because it's the truth. That's what people would be seeing. I just didn't keep it a secret. There are many things like that you can say or do that are mostly dictated by the friendly relationship you develop.

The point is that the salesperson that hears, "No" when they first ask a customer to sit on the bike but gets them to sit on it anyway will also be a good salesperson at the write-up and closing stages. These really do have a lot in common. I am sure you understand all of the benefits to having a dreamer sitting on their dream bike.

The salespeople who are having difficulty with this step then how much more will they have problems with the up-coming steps? For the most part it is a lack of confidence in them-selves. They are still afraid to be in control. They need to roll play with another salesperson on how simple it is to get a customer to sit on a motorcycle that they have been dreaming about for a long time.

Roll playing with someone else is the best way I know of to sharpen your skills. When you are done role playing, let the other person critique you. Then swap positions and roll play again. Now you offer them your advice and opinion. Besides picking up helpful hints from your partner you are also teaching yourself by offering wise advice.

Chapter Five
How Much Is It

Note:

When you are first asked for the selling price of a model, a really good answer would be to give a price range. For example, if the base price of a particular motorcycle was 15,995 you might answer by saying something like,

"The price ranges from fifteen nine to seventeen five. It just depends upon how you have it equipped."............ I have a lot more to say about that answer in the up-coming pages.

My point is that sooner or later an exact price comes into play. In the following chapter in order to simplify things, I am going to use a starting price so that I can make some valuable points clear. I am confident that you will know how to mix my information into your price quoting procedure.

How Much Is It

If you think about all the things people want, more than likely the only reason they don't have them is, they have to pay for them first. This one little ole reason is preventing them from having whatever they want. If the money problem is solved, everyone would own what they want and I am sure you would too. Be it a bicycle, motorcycle, car, airplane, yacht or anything else you wanted.

When I do sales training for experienced sales people, I always ask them this question. What are the reasons your customers gave you for not trying to buy today? I can always count on getting these four answers.

They have to talk to their spouse

They want to shop around first

They want to think about it

They are waiting for things like taxes or their house to sell

I always get animated at this point and jump up and down and say that balloons are falling from the ceiling. That the band begins to play and a girl pops out of a cake holding a big sign that reads;

Congratulations!!! You are the one millionth-customer that said that they have to talk to their wife before they buy.

She then says, "For being the one millionth customer who said that, the price of the motorcycle is no longer $15,995, but it is now only $15.95. Just sixteen dollars total delivered out the door. Wow!!! We are so happy for you!!! But there are two rules."

"Rule number 1. You only get ten seconds to make up your mind. The clock is ticking do you want it for $15.95. Tick…Tick. Yes you do!!!" Alright! Now for rule number 2."

"Oh no….. Bummer……Rule number 2 says that the only one who can't get this super deal is a liar, and sir, you just made a decision without talking to your wife. You lied to us! We must ask you to leave the premises.

So if you understand what my point is to that silly story then you will realize that the problem really is not that they need to talk to the spouse. Heck, they have been talking to each other since they first met. The *real problem* is we need to bring the conversation to what the *real problem is* and then doing all we can to make the price affordable.

Think about those four answers. The customer who wants to talk to their spouse is going to talk to them about money.

The Customer who wants to go home and think about it is going to think about the money.

The customer who wants to shop around is trying to save money.

The customer who is waiting is waiting for money.

Let's do a roll play about answering the question of how much is it? I am going to start and stop the role play a few times and then always start back at the beginning because I believe so much that you need to totally understand how this procedure will get a lot of motorcycles purchased from you and a lot of customers affordably living the dream.

Customer John: "So Steve, how much is it?"

Steve: "Well John the price of this bike is only nineteen-five-fifty ($19,550) and that's a lot of bike for the money."

Time Out

When I am doing seminars I ask the salespeople attending why they should say, "Only" in front of the price?" The audience normally says that it makes the price seem lower. I reply, "Nope, it doesn't."

I don't care if I go back to 1972 when I sold my first bike, a Trail Hopper Suzuki for $295.00. When I said only in front of the price, the customer grimaced a bit and said, "Yea, right, only."

At this point of the seminar I take my cup of coffee and start spraying it around the room and letting it splash on the hotel meeting room carpet. The crowed normally gets a shocked look on their faces and start chuckling. I ask them what that is. I can count on hearing things like weird and strange but finally someone says, "its coffee on the carpet."

I say, "No. It's 'Only' coffee on the carpet."

Do you know why it is 'Only' coffee on the carpet........Because it is not my carpet. I would never dump coffee on purpose on my own carpet.

The point is whenever you are talking about the customers' money, be it the price of the bike, down payment, monthly payments or during the negotiation stage, you must say 'Only', or 'Just' before saying the money amount. If you get a sour look face or have a quiver in your tone and show fear and it is not your money, how in the world can the customer feel good about it when it is their money? It should also be your mission to soften the price by having an 'Only' mannerism while discussing money.

When I do experienced salespeople training, I could tell that they were ready for my question of "How much is it?" One or two people blurt out, " It's only $15,995. Then they stop talking and smile waiting for a verbal pat on the back.

That's a terrible answer I respond. I then explain the power of the zipper. The zipper is your mouth and the power is when and where you zip it.

We already know that for the most part, the money is the only reason people do not buy what they want. It is such a disservice to leave someone at the worst place you can be at by saying the 'Only' price then hitting the zipper. What is the customer supposed to say? One of the most common replies is, "Is that your best price?" The salesman normally says no and then offers a discounted price. The customer was willing to pay full price but now the salesperson has created a discount buyer.

Time In

Customer John: "So, Steve how much is it?"

Salesman Steve: "John, the price is only nineteen-five-fifty and that's a lot of bike for the money. The best part John is you don't have to pay for it....well not all at once anyway. John we have some awesome financing and we can really make it easy and affordable to take home. Were you planning on financing the motorcycle?"

"Yes I am. I was planning on putting two thousand down. What would my payment be?"

Time Out

If you think about most conversations, you will realize that the listener will continue the conversation where the talker stopped. It is just human nature. So by simply quoting the *Only* price, then in the same mannerism continue talking by switching the conversation to your great financing, many times you will find that their next response is, "What would my payments be?"

Yes. Some customers will switch you back to the money and want a better price. This is not all bad. Now you are in a position to sit down and begin a write-up. If all goes well, you will end up with an offer to buy today.

Customer John: "So, Steve how much is it?"

Salesman Steve: "John, the price is only nineteen-five-fifty and that's a lot of bike for the money. The best part John is you don't have to pay for it....well not all at once anyway. John we have some awesome financing and can really make it easy and affordable to take home. Were you planning on financing the motorcycle?"

John: "Yes I am. I was planning on putting two thousand down. What would my payment be?"

Steve: "John, one of the reasons I said we have awesome financing is that we work with many lenders. Let's go have a seat and I will explain our cool method of financing." Turn and walk to your desk.

Steve: "Ok John, here's how our financing works. We quite honestly could get you over a hundred different payments for the same motorcycle. But you know the best payment is the one that works for you. John, what payment would fit your budget? Some people like to pay the bike off early and get payments around $600.00 is that what you're thinking?"

John: "No Steve that would be way too high."

Steve: "No problem John. That would be way too high for me too. What payment would work for you? $500...$450...$425..."

John: "Gee Steve, I was hoping to get a payment around $300. Do you think that is possible?"

Steve: "I sure do, John. We are definitely in the ball park. Tell you what. Let me get a little bit of information from you and then I can get you an exact payment quote to the penny. John, who is the first person you are going to show your new motorcycle to?"

Time Out

I am not only switching the conversation from the money but I am also trying to have them visualize themselves showing the motorcycle to a relative or friend. I am also hoping to get some good leads. You should always ask every customer if they know someone looking for a new motorcycle. Many, many times you will end up with several names and phone numbers to prospect with. The beauty of that is you can use your customer's name as a reference, making it much easier to get a good friendly conversation going.

As a young salesman I ended up getting 11 sales because one customer purchased from me and gave me three references. Two of the references purchased a new motorcycle and the reference circle continued to 11 sold units. Most of them happened in a 30-day period.

For most customers the price it not the main issue. You could sell many people a motorcycle for a million dollars if you had a payment of ten dollars a month. I hope you believe that.

Asking the customer what payment is affordable is the key to switching from the higher price they are not paying to the smaller affordable price they are going to pay. I mean, really, how far apart can you be on a payment? Once you get the payment that the customer can afford you are more than likely going to close the purchase.

When the customer asks the price, this is the best time to answer it and then switch the conversation to financing. If the customer gives you a payment that works for them, you will find that most of the time price is no longer the issue.

On average 80% of the customers finance their purchase either with you or their own lender. If the customer's payment is $300.00 per month, then it only cost $10.00 a day to buy the motorcycle of their dreams. Most people sell or trade their bike within three years and will get around 60% to 70% of their purchase price back. That would mean to live the dream would cost them only 30% - 40% of their payment or just $3.00 - $4.00 a day. That's less than a Big Mac. Do you think your customer would rather have the motorcycle of their dreams today or a Big Mac? How about tomorrow? How about next week? Amazing isn't it? These numbers are easy to understand because it is the simple truth. The secret is to not keep it a secret and share the information with every customer. Living the dream really is very affordable.

To be able to talk about the monthly and the daily price of a bike is greatly increased by the step-two relationship you developed before price was even brought up. Probing is such a big part of the selling process and so is switching from price to finance.

I hope you noticed two things.

1.   I never quoted a payment. Heck, that's not my job.

2.   What I did do was ask the customer what payment worked for them. But I hope you also noticed that I started at the higher payment of $600.00. Believe it or not, sometimes the customer says that the payment $600.00 a month works for them But most customers will say that $600.00 is too high. So the next step is to come down in small increments.

Many times the customer has a payment range. They might be thinking $300-$350. If you asked what payment they wanted without starting high, you will almost always hear the lower amount of $300.00. But if you start your suggestion payment high and you come down in small increments, you will almost always get the higher payment request of $350.00. If it is possible to get the lower payment I am sure the customer won't mind; but if it needs to be higher, than the payment range will be very helpful.

Chapter Six
Asking For the Sale

It is amazing how many times I have witnessed a salesperson spend a lot of time with a customer and never got around to asking for the sale. I suppose they are waiting for the customer to say, "Ok, I want to buy one."

You might think that it would be good if all your customers were easy to sell, but think about it. If all the customers were that easy, why would the dealership need salespeople? The customer could just take the tag off of the bike and bring it up to the counter to complete the sale. So every customer who has some objections for you to overcome should almost get a hand shake and a sincere thank you, because if not for them, you might not have a job.

Every customer needs to be asked to buy several times. If it is done right, you will either get a positive answer of yes or you will get some key information and be in a position to overcome the objection and write up the deal.

Even if they do not buy today, you will be a lot more informed when you do a follow-up call. The more you and the customer get to know each other, the more information you get, the more likely they will buy from you. Getting good information definitely increases the chances for a sale.

My brother Ed taught me at the young age of 18 to ask for the sale early. He taught me a very easy greeting that also includes asking for the sale.

"Hi folks, how are you doing? Do you see one you would like to take home with you today?"

Many times I heard, "Yes there is, we would like to see what kind of deal / payment we can get on a......."

Now to be honest most of the time they will not say yes. You will get the standard reply of, "No thanks, just looking." Ok, strike one, but that is all it is. Just like in Baseball you get three strikes until you are out; and if you foul off the last pitch you get to keep swinging. Sometimes you might ask for the sale 10 times or more. The better you develop the relationship the more swings you will get to take.

The two most common comments the customers will say are:

"Just looking"

"How much is it?"

When they ask the price this might a good time to ask for the sale. If you feel you have made a strong enough connection with the customer, you might answer the question something like this:

"The price is only $12,900 (To be said short form. The price is only twelve-nine) and that's a super price. The really good news is we have awesome financing. Would you like to sit down and see how low we can get the payments?"

Most of the sales are being financed. Be it by you or an outside lender or possibly it will be a cash sale. You will in most instances find out the answer if you ask them if they want to sit down and see how low they can get their payment. They will normally at the least let you know how they would pay for it.

As unlikely as this will sound, the number one mistake made by salespeople is that they don't ask for the sale. Here's the reason. They act like salespeople. A salesperson tries to sell you something. If the customer doesn't buy, that's it – he quits, he's out of bullets. Their downfall is that they get enough sales to get by, so they feel they have an okay system.

It's their Bus Stop, or in other words their life and I'm not going to rain on their Stop; but I'm here to tell you it is not an okay way to go about it, not by a long shot. Good luck trying to intimidate or lean on customers to buy. You will get some sales that way, but I don't like your chances for repeat business or referrals.

What I'm about to say demonstrates once again the tremendous difference between a salesperson and a Help-You-Buy Person. Like a salesperson, the Help-You-Buy Person wants the sale and if he or she is any good at all, he wants it today.

To make this happen, there are some things you need to know. You've got to know that if they do buy today, they do so because they wanted too. Also, you've got to believe that the customer is there because you have something they want.

You've got to believe that your company wants them to make the purchase. You've got to know why you are there, which is to help them buy what they want. And both you and the customer must know that they don't have to pay for it, not all at once anyway, because you have a super financing program. And most important of all, if your customer doesn't say they will buy one today, then you *Gotta* ask for the sale.

When you ask for the sale one of two things will happen. They will either try to buy, or they won't. I am not concerned at this time with which one it is. We will be dealing with both decisions later. My concern right now is that you understand that you must ask for the sale from *every single customer you encounter*.

When you play Talk Ping-Pong with your customers by asking WHAT questions and then hitting your zipper, you will become a friend in the business instead of a salesperson. Now, how tough is it to ask a friend, "Would you like to buy one today?" Believe it or not, this is the question *least* asked in sales situations.

The best outcome, of course, is when the customer says, "Yes!"

What's the worst thing that can happen?

It's not that they may say "No!"

The worst thing that can happen is that you don't ask at all. Because if you do ask and they say no, then you can put on your Sherlock Holmes hat and get to work solving the mystery of *The Customer Who Didn't Buy What He Wants*. And just think, what if you do discover the answer, then solve the problem, and your new friend buys what they want? Who's the winner? Who helped them win? Gosh, what a friend you are! You didn't quit. You hung in there and helped someone have a better Bus Stop. You should almost feel guilty about getting paid. Well...we won't go that far. Still, it's a great job –making people happy, helping them buy what they want – not like real work at all.

The second thing that makes it easy is the Gotta-Wanna. If you *want* to ask, you will. Try it with me one time. Say the following line out loud: "Would you like to see how easily you can take it home today?" How does that sound? Say it again. Practice it.

Being a top Help-You-Buy Person is simple. Take it one step at a time, say the words you already know, and apply the Gotta-Wanna we were all born with. You have now mixed the ingredients for the simplest formula there is for success.

In the early 70's I met a customer who became, and is still, a good friend of mine today. His name is Chuck Rushton. Chuck came in one day and we had a lot of fun talking about different things. We shared some jokes and lied to each other about our love lives. I was so sure that he would come back and buy a motorcycle from me that I bet my brother Ed $10.00 that he would.

Well, I was half-right. He did come back. He came back to show me the motorcycle he bought from another dealership. He must have spent an hour telling me how much more he liked me then the guy he bought it from. He went on and on about how much he had wanted to buy one from me. He explained that he was giving a friend from work a ride home when they drove past the other dealership. He said all he intended to do was show his friend what he was going to buy from me. He told me that the salesperson just sat there like a bump on a log not saying anything at all except answering questions he was asked. But when Chuck and his friend were ready to leave, he did ask him if there was anything he could do that would make him want to buy it today.

"Sure," Chuck said, "Get my payments under $150.00." The next thing he knew he was sitting in the office signing an offer sheet and before he knew it he was signing a contract.

Then Chuck had the nerve to tell me his payment ended up being $190.00. I could have easily got that payment for him, or possibly less. I couldn't believe that he thought that was funny. He apologized and said that he just got hung up on the excitement of buying one, something he'd been dreaming about for so long.

I said, "Gee, Chuck, why didn't you buy one from me?"

He replied, "You didn't ask."

That was the greatest commission I never made. I explained to my brother Ed how the light came on, that I learned my lesson. (He still made me pay him the ten bucks. He was a hard guy to get a break from on a bet.)

The lesson I learned that day has saved a countless number of my new friends from buying from the wrong person at the wrong place. I knew at the time that Chuck was a buyer. I just didn't understand what my main job was at the time – to ask for the sale. It is so simple once you understand

Once you have a good relationship with the customer and have gone over the price and your super financing, simply say something like, "Let's go sit down and figure out the details? I know they can make it extremely affordable. It's possible you might be able to take it home today." Then turn and walk to your desk or seating area.

Sometimes the customer declines to go with you. When that does happen, they normally give you an objection why not. Now at the least you're in a position to try and solve it. But then again…Sometimes they do go with you and you get a write-up. Either way you can't lose. You might not get the sale but winning and losing are not based on the results. It is based on good quality efforts. You can't make the buying decision for the customer but you can 100% give it your best shot to help them buy.

When you mention price and switch to finance, you will often be asked how much the payment would be or how much down payment is needed. Sometimes you get asked both. This is a total buying signal and of course you should say something like, "No problem. Let's go have a

48

seat. I just need to get a little information first and then I will get you those answers."

When a discount request is made like, "What's your best price?" You can follow up with, "Let's go sit down and figure that out. One thing I know for sure is that they will do all they can to make you happy."

Or maybe the customer offers you a discounted price. Always remember this rhyme, DON'T FIGHT IT.......WRITE IT. So of course you would say something like, "Hey, we're definitely in the ball park. Let's go have a seat and I will take the offer to my manager."

One of the best ways I know of is to say, at the right time, "Would you like to see how easy it is to take one home today?" If the answer is "Yes," you will end up sitting down with your customer and filling out a write-up form.

If the answer is "No" and your customer says, "I'll be back", then this is a perfect time to bring him to your desk to get them a card and go over a few things. A great question to ask at that time would be:

"What's stopping you from buying today?" By doing so you just might solve the problem on the spot.

I already went over the four most common responses of: wife, shop, think and waiting. After you get an answer like that or a similar one, you can follow up by saying, "Is it a matter of which bike to get, the price, the down payment or the monthly payments?" You are now trying to bring out the truth of the objection by switching to the money. Preferably it will be the smaller monthly payment. Whatever their answer is, you should do what I call, *"If we could, would you?"*

"If we could get you that price, would you like to buy it today?"

"If we could get you that payment, would you like to buy it today?"

"If we could get you your requested down payment, would you like to buy it today?"

"If we could make you happy on your trade value, would you like to buy it today?"

Let's say that customer Mike wanted to talk to his wife before he made a buying decision. You can follow that comment up with something like:

Salesperson; "Great Mike, I do understand that. I like to talk to my (wife-husband-parents) too before I make a big decision. What do you think she will care about most? Is it which bike to get, the price, down payment or monthly payments?"

Customer Mike: "She takes care of all our bills so the down payment and monthly payment would be her greatest concern."

Salesperson: "That's good. You want to make sure you can afford it. You know we have some awesome financing. We can normally get a payment that works for most people. How much were you thinking about putting down?"

Customer Mike: "Oh, somewhere around $1,000."

Salesperson: "Cool, that shouldn't be a problem. What payment would work best for you? Some people like to pay it off early and have higher payments around $600.00. Is that what you were thinking?"

Customer Mike: "Oh gosh no, that would be way out of my budget."

Salesperson: "Well, Mike, we have very flexible financing. What payment would work for you? Would $500.00 do the trick.............No, well what would work? Would $450 a month make you want to take it home?................How about $400.00?"

You can keep going down to the point of being almost ridiculous. You are not saying you can get those payments. You are saying that you will try to get them a payment that will fit their budget. This way, if they don't buy today, and they go home and talk to their spouse they will tell them how cool we are and that we will do our best to make them happy.

At the time of purchase there is a good chance that they will get their desired payment. If not, you will never be far apart. You have now taken the higher price of the motorcycle and reduced it to the much lower difference in payment. You made it easy to buy.

Time In

Customer Mike: "No, we were thinking about somewhere in the neighborhood of $300."

Salesperson: "Well Mike we are definitely in the ball park. Say, IF WE COULD GET THAT PAYMENT, WOULD YOU LIKE TO TAKE IT HOME WITH YOU?"

That was an example of: "*If we could, would you?*" Whatever the objection is, you are always in position to say, "If we could solve that problem, would you like to take it home?" If they say yes, you would then write it up and take the problem to the sales manager. Now together you have a buyer and if you can solve the problem or compromise with the buyer, you end up with a happy customer living the dream and you made it happen.

Time Out

Whenever I am teaching or writing I can always close the sale but in this situation I am not going to close it. The customer is going to go home and talk it over with his wife.

Time In

Customer Mike: "No, I still need to talk it over with her. Do you have a card and I will be back."

Salesperson: "I sure do, Mike. Okay, here's my card. Mike, I do hope you know that we really do want your business. Is there anything we can do now to earn it today?"

Customer Mike: "No, I need to go over the information with my wife first."

Salesperson: "I understand what you are saying Mike. You don't want to go home with a new motorcycle to find out you don't have a wife. (Ha-ha-ha.) No sale is worth that. But Mike is there a payment that would work for you today? How about $275.00? ...Would $250.00 do the trick?"

Customer Mike: "Nope. I gotta talk it over with her first no matter what."

Salesperson: "Ok Mike. Please do. But there are three things I hope you know about the dealership and me. The first thing is that we don't tell people what their payment has to be. We work hard to get the payment that works best for our customers. We will be more than happy to go to bat for you. We can't always get it but we can always try."

"The second thing I want you to know about us is that we really do want your business. We will always do our best to earn it. When your wife and you have figured out what payment range fits your budget, please let us know and we will do all we can to get it for you." And if any questions should pop up, please don't hesitate to give me a call."

"The third thing is, Mike we provide super service after the sale. We feel if we make you happy enough to buy here and keep you happy with our service after the sale you will be a loyal customer. We will try just as hard after the sale to keep you happy as we did while you are purchasing it. If we do all that Mike, would you stay our friend and think of us as your dealership?"

Customer Mike: "I sure would. You have been so much easier to talk to than the last place I went to. I got the feeling they did not care if I got one from them. You can count on the fact that when I get one I will buy it from you."

Salesperson: "Thank you Mike. It has been my pleasure working with you and I really do look forward to the big smile you will have on your face when you ride your new motorcycle off of the showroom floor. Mike, we have a lot of rides, events and barbeques at the dealership. Let me get your number and email so I can log it into the computer to make sure you get informed about them."

Now you are not only in a position to inform them about your events but you can also follow-up with a phone call from time to time to see how the buying decision is going and answer any questions that might have come up.

Also notice I did not say, "Can I get your phone number?" I think that question makes people feel a bit uncomfortable. What I did say was, "Let me get your phone number." You will find that you will almost always get the number when you say it like that.

It's very important that you take the time to sit down with every customer you believe is in the market for your product, which should be most of them. This is why I prefer to leave my cards at my desk. It's not very hard to get a friend to walk over to your desk in order to get a card and talk about a few things – a few very important, truthful things, the most important being "What's stopping you from buying today?"

Let's discuss sitting at the desk a bit more. It seems that every time I give a seminar to experienced salespeople and I say that at least 80 % of your customers should sit at your desk, I hear, "No way." They say to me, "Steve, maybe that works in the big cities, but this is a little town, and you can't do that high of a percentage with our customers."

When I'm in the big city, I hear how it might work like that in hick towns but the city folks would never go for it. No matter where I am, I always hear you can't do that high of a percentage in their city. They say that their customers would never go for it.

I don't get it. First of all, what do they mean by *my customer* won't go for it? Go for *what*? I just want to sit down with my friend and make sure we've gone over everything. It's no big deal.

To prove my point, I have some fun with the group. I tell them I've been secretly working on a new pay plan with their manager. Since they didn't believe they were capable of getting 80% of their customers to sit down, we were going to convert them to Liners and hire Closers to come in behind them and close the sale. Their only job would be to greet customers, find out what they are interested in, and sit them down in the office. When that happens, the Closer will take his shot at making the deal.

I like to pause for a second or two at this point and look at the daggers in their eyes as they stare back at me. I don't pause for too long because I get scared I might start actually feeling those daggers. So I tell them the good news. I explain that after the Closer comes into the office, the salesperson who sat his customer down goes to his manager's office and gets a $100 bill. Every time one of their customers sits down at the salesperson's desk, they get $100. Even if the customer doesn't try to buy, the salesperson still gets paid.

By this time the daggers are no longer there. They are replaced with cash register eyes. I can almost hear the sound of little bells as they ring up their sit-downs. I then ask them how much money they would average if they greeted ten customers a day. I hear $1,000 from most of them, a few say $900, and one or two say $800.

I pause again, and then look at them funny.

It takes a second or two.

Then they start laughing.

They realize that their excuses just flew out the window. All of a sudden they went from being negative about the 80% sit-down to becoming positive that they could do it. Many of them said that they could do better than what I said they should. Why? It's because they just tapped into the power that they always had. They just went from a mowing-the-lawn attitude to a playing-a-game attitude. They tapped into their Gotta-Wanna. Now they *wanted* to sit those customers down at their desks, and that made all the difference.

Unfortunately for them, I was only kidding about the pay plan. But it was very fortunate for them if they understood what just took place and committed to applying what they just realized. In order to sell more bikes you must write-up more customers. In order to write-up more customers you must sit more customers down. It will always work like that. Also if the customer does sit down with you but does not try to buy the motorcycle, your chances of getting him back in the store has doubled.

This happens because most customers really do appreciate that you took the time to sit down with them. If they do shop around, it would be easy to understand why more customers will choose buying from you than the salesperson who only tried to sell the bike. You really can create very loyal customers if you build a great relationship.

Chapter Seven
The Write-Up Commitment

Note:

     I mentioned in the beginning of this book I would be using some of the material that was in my first book: You Gotta-Wanna. From the first day the write-up and closing procedures were invented until the end of time not many things are going to change about them. It is all about getting the commitment before we negotiate. Yes, you can bring in a filled out work sheet to talk to your boss trying to get a price, trade or payment quote but that is wonderment, not a write-up. Once the customer commits to a solid figure then the work sheet becomes a write-up.

     I did edit and delete some of the material and I added several more concepts. Even if you have read it before I am certain you will gain valuable information because it has probably been awhile since you read it so it will be a good refresher. Also the new material will definitely give you some good ideas to think about. If you did not read my first book, then it will all be new information to you.

The Write Up

A write-up is a signed, committed offer to do
business today. As simple as that sounds, many salespeople don't
understand that. Most of their confusion comes from the words
committed offer. They think if the customer's only concern is getting the
best price or how much the payments are going to be and then want to
go home and think about it, that they have a write-up. They think if they
write down the customer's question and ask the boss for the answer, they
have a write-up.

Wrong. These are not write-ups. It's a good beginning; but if you are
only answering questions without obtaining the commitment, you are
actually being an information broker. Hopefully you will use that
information to sit the customer down and find out whatever it would
take to get a commitment from them to buy today.

Your mindset needs to be that 100% of the time there's got to be a
way the customer would buy what they have been dreaming about.
There has got to be a way to get them to live the dream.

There is no such thing as a ridiculous offer. I had many in my day.
Yes, many of them did not turn into a sale, but then again, many did.
Getting the first offer is usually the hardest one. Now that the customer
has made an offer they are in the buying mode. And of course they know
their offer was ridiculous. More than likely they are prepared to spend
more than they offered. It's just their way of playing the game.

I would make a bet that the salesperson that got the most ridiculous
offers to buy also had the most total write-ups by month's end. You see,
when you are good at getting any offer, you become great at getting
quality offers. Of course it will almost always hold true, the salesperson
who got the most write-ups took home the biggest pay check.

Roger Cooper

I want to tell you a little bit about one of the best friends I have ever had. His name is Roger Cooper. I will be using Roger in the roll plays that are soon to follow.

In 1972 I went to work for my brother Ed at his dealership called Albany Suzuki. It took me awhile but I became the top salesman every month beating out four other salespeople. Well, for eight months straight I did.

Then one day Ed hired a few more salespeople. One of them was a goofy character by the name of Roger Cooper.

Cooper had been working in the Oregon woods as a choker setter. He manhandled a massive chain around huge downed trees then helped pull them up the hill. It was backbreaking, dangerous work. When I shook his coarse and scabby hand for the first time, I remember thinking, "I can't believe Ed hired this bozo."

Well guess what? Roger kicked my butt his very first month. I could not believe it, but then Ed explained to me what I was doing wrong and my sales almost doubled after that.

You see, I thought I knew who was a buyer and who could afford to buy. I was not being a salesperson. I had become a sales consultant…A sales skimmer. Without realizing it I was talking people out of buying.

Roger didn't know any better so he just simply wrote everybody up. Roger's passion was motorcycles and he truly loved seeing the look on his buyer's face as they rode home on their new bike.

From that day until I was promoted to sales manager I found a way to write-up a high percentage of the customers I talked to. I finally understood that once you get the first offer to buy, the customer's excitement level increases. The write-up does most of the work. What we were apart in price, trade or payments was a much smaller percentage than the original offer so we closed the deal many times.

The reason why Roger Cooper beat me in his first month on the job was he just did what my brother Ed told him to do, step-by-step, and wrote his customers up with depressing regularity. Depressing for me, that is, not for Cooper or my brother. But then Ed told me in advance what was going to happen and it did.

Cooper had the normal sophomore slump and ended up in fifth place his second month. Cooper thought Ed's advice was for beginners and he got smarter than the write-up. Roger figured out his mistake quicker than I did and the two of us had many fearsome battles at being salesman of the month.

As an example, let's do some more role-playing. This first example will show what Cooper was like his first month. The next will show what Cooper became during his second month.

We will start halfway through the probe. Cooper is dealing with a customer who is paying cash.

"So, Roger," Cooper's customer says, "is seventy-five-fifty your best price?"

"Really, Frank, it's a super price and we have some of the best financing in the world. I'm sure we can work out some affordable payments," Cooper says, expecting Frank to ask how much the payment is going to be.

"I'll be paying cash," Frank boasts with a broad smile. "If we can work out a deal, I'll leave you a deposit and bring in the balance when I pick up the bike. Would you take sixty-eight hundred for it?"

"Sixty-eight hundred," Cooper repeats out loud, and then says, "Wow, that really would be a super price. *If we could get that price would you* like to take it home with you today?"

"If you can go that price, I'll buy it today," Frank says with the pride of being a buyer and not just a looker.

"Well, the worst thing that can happen is that the boss says no. Let's go find out." As Cooper finishes his last statement, he turns and walks into his office with Frank following him. Roger sits down, fills out the write-up form, then turns it around and reads it to Frank. He then asks, "Is that right?"

Frank agrees. "If they go for that price, I'll take it home today."

"Great," Cooper says sincerely, "I just need you to okay the offer here." Cooper hands Frank a pen while pointing out where to sign it. After Frank approves his offer, he breathes a sigh of relief.

"Super, I'll give it my best shot, Wish me luck," Cooper says and then holds out his hand for Frank to shake.

"Good luck," Franks says. Cooper turns and hustles out to his manager.

This is a write-up. We have a committed offer to do business today. Later we'll talk about how we could have made it a stronger offer by getting the down payment, but for now we'll stick with the write-up.

Let's see the difference between this write-up and Cooper's approach during his second month.

"So, Roger, is seventy-five fifty your best price?" Cooper's customer asks.

"Really Frank, it's a super price and we have some of the best financing in the world. I'm sure we can work out some affordable payments," Cooper says, expecting Frank to ask how much the payment will be.

"I'll be paying cash," Frank boasts with a broad smile. "If we can work out a deal, I'll leave you a deposit and bring in the balance when I pick up the bike. Would they take sixty-eight hundred for it?"

"Sixty-eight hundred," Cooper repeats out loud. "No. There's no way I could get you that price. I had two customers buy one of those last week. The best price I could get for them is seventy-two hundred. Did you want to buy one at that price?"

"No, I think I'll shop around first. If I can't beat that price I'll be back," Frank says, a little disappointed that he couldn't get his price, and that Cooper didn't even attempt to get him his offer.

Cooper's the bad guy salesperson instead of the good guy Help-You-Buy Person.

"Okay," Cooper responds, "see what you can do and if you can't beat it, come on back and ask for me and I will get you the price we talked about." Roger had become smarter than a write-up.

A VERY COMMON HAPPENING among salespeople is they become what I call sales advisors or consultants. They start informing their customers what they have to do to buy instead of finding what it would take to earn their business today. The two steps that you must understand and accomplish properly to be a top salesperson are the probe and the write-up.

You've seen what a write-up is – Cooper his first month on the job – now let's talk about what a write-up does. A write-up separates what we don't *have* to talk about and lets us focus on what we do *need* to talk about.

In the first example, when Cooper took the write-up to the sales manager, we had a committed offer at $6,800. The original price was $7,550. That meant the customer wanted a $750 discount. It also means that we no longer have to worry about the majority of the price. Now we have taken care of $6,800 so we only have $750 left to handle. You are now nearly 90 percent of the way home. Put another way, you have taken 90 percent of the price and eliminated it, leaving only ten percent left to solve between you, the sales manager, and the customer.

61

If you hadn't written it up, you would be forced to negotiate the entire price at once. I'd much rather try to solve a $750 problem than a $7,550 problem. When you try to solve a big problem, you put a lot more pressure on the customer to make a total decision all at once instead of taking it one step at a time.

Maybe the sales manager will approve the offer on the spot – maybe he won't discount it a penny. I say *maybe* because we are speaking of results. These decisions are in the manager's control. Don't worry about what he will do. He has a number of factors going into his decisions, factors that can change from day to day and about which you know nothing about. Concentrate your efforts on what you do and strive to get write-ups!

In Cooper's second scenario, we ended up with our product still on the show room floor and a customer driving to the competition at Cooper's invitation.

Let's see, we have a choice of a customer driving down the road with us being $7,550 apart, or we could have Frank sitting in the office inches away from becoming an owner and experiencing those Cloud Nine feelings. We are only $750 apart. Now you, your sales manager, and the customer (who's first offer is often less than what they expect to pay) are now in a position to come up with many options to overcome the objection. This should not be a tough choice and should be easy to understand.

It should now be clear not only what a write-up is but also what it does and why it works. I can sum up everything in these few words: Don't Fight it; Write it.

WHENEVER I FINISHED TRAINING groups of new salespeople at Ed's dealership in Oregon, he would join us and say, "I want to be sure that Steve made one thing very clear. If a customer comes in and says he will buy a new motorcycle if my wife will run away with him and you don't bring me the offer, I will fire you. They are my motorcycles and my wife let me decide which deal I want. I will probably say no to the offer, I am pretty fond of my wife but let me decide what is most important. This way we will be in a position to make a counter offer.

Maybe he would settle for a cute picture of her. If you don't bring the offer to buy, I can't help you solve the problem."

Ed was just having some fun. He wanted all the new salespeople to know that *there is no objection* to getting a write-up. There is not an offer too ridiculous to be considered. The worst thing that can happen is the deal is not made. You lost nothing but you did gain valuable experience. Believe me that many ridiculous offers will turn into sales.

The main reason we have salespeople is *not* to sell. Their number one reason for being on the job is to find what it would take to make a customer happy enough to try and buy what they want. The results are the children of your efforts. I guarantee in the long run that the salesperson who delivered the most products also had the most write-ups.

Remember, you're a Help-You-Buy Person. The average customer would love to have what they want especially when they are looking at it. This is where Sherlock Holmes comes back into the picture. If they want to buy, then be a nice Help-You-Buy Person and write them up. But if they don't try to buy what they want, obviously there's a reason. Now it's time for you to become like Sherlock Holmes and find the mystery of why someone wouldn't try to buy what they want. Then remember: IF We Could Would You? Always be looking for a way to write it up.

Let's go back to Roger Cooper's role playing. This time we will do it completely right by trying to get the down payment with the offer. Please note I said *trying* to get the down payment. The name of the sales game is controlling your efforts then watching the birth of your results.

I'm going to start the role play from the beginning. Work with me. Each time you go through it you will pick up something new. Read and grow. Your eyes will do the work.

"So, Roger," Cooper's customer says, "is seventy-five fifty your best price?"

"Really, Frank, it's a super price and we have some of the best financing in the world. I'm sure we can work out some affordable payments," Cooper says, expecting Frank to ask how much the payment is going to be.

"I'll be paying cash," Frank boasts with a broad smile. "If we can work out a deal, I'll leave you a deposit and bring in the balance when I pick up the bike. Would you take sixty-eight hundred for it?" Frank asks, secretly hoping that Cooper won't accept his offer because then he will feel he offered too much.

"Sixty-eight hundred," Cooper repeats out loud, and then says, "Wow, that really would be a super price. *If we could get that price, would you* like to take it home with you today?"

"If you can go that price, I'll buy it today," Frank says with the pride of being a buyer and not just a looker.

"Well, the worst thing that can happen is that the boss says no. Let's go find out." As Cooper finishes his last statement, he turns and walks into his office with Frank following him. Roger sits down, fills out the write-up form then turns it around and reads it to Frank. He then asks, "Is that right?"

Frank agrees, saying once again, "If they go for that price, I'll take it home today."

"Great," Cooper says sincerely, "I just need you to okay the offer here." Cooper hands Frank a pen while pointing out where to sign it. After Frank approves his offer, he breathes a sigh of relief.

"Frank," Cooper asks, "Is your down payment going to be cash or check?"

"It'll be a check," Frank replies.

"Super," Roger says with approval. "Go ahead and write a check and I'll take it in with me."

If you do it this way, over half of all customers will pull out their checkbook and write a check for the down payment without a word. Simply put, by making it a statement instead of a question what you're doing is avoiding any objections. Sometimes if you ask someone to do something and then take a defensive role by explaining why you asked, you create an objection. Many times this would not have happened if you just assumed they would do as you stated instead of asking.

But sometimes this is the way it happens:

"Super," Roger says with approval. "Go ahead and write a check and I'll take it in with me."

Instead of pulling out his checkbook, the customer says, "Tell you what, Roger, why don't you go see if they will take my offer, then I'll write you a check. There's not much sense in writing out a check just to find out they won't take the offer."

"I understand what you're saying Frank, but that's not in your best interest," Cooper explains. "Frank, I've got to go into my boss and ask him to take $750 and throw it out the window. I know you love that idea but my boss never jumps up and down with excitement about knocking money off. From his point of view, I can't blame him, though I can see it's a great idea from your point of view.

You see, if I go in with just the offer, the manager will look at it – We don't need your money to show the boss you're serious. We know you would not go this far if you weren't serious. But tell me this Frank, which one is harder to say no to?"

Cooper picks up the write-up then continues. "If you were the boss and I brought this offer the way it is? Or if I brought you the offer and the down payment to you at the same time, if I stuck the money in your hand, wouldn't it be harder to turn down?"

"Yeah, it sure would," Frank replies.

"All right then," Cooper says with his patented smile. "Help me to help you, and write a check and I'll take it in with the deal."

That was always one of my favorite things to say at the right time. "Help me to help you." It is 100% the truth. I sincerely want to help them to have a better time at their Bus Stop. It all comes down to the reality that the winner is the buyer and I want to help them to win. The fact is that 75% of the deals that come in with a down payment end up being a sale. That is an amazingly high percentage.

Here is another example of overcoming the objection of the down payment:

"Frank, let's say you were trying to sell your own car. You had a for-sale sign in the window asking $3,000. You get a telephone call and they offer you $2,600 for it. You think about it for a second then turn down the offer. Now the phone rings again and this time someone offers you $2,550 for it. Well, you already turned down more so you turn that offer down as well. Then there is a knock on the door. When you open it you find someone holding $2,500 in their hand. They give you the money to hold while you consider his offer. Which offer would be the hardest to turn down?" I let the customer picture the scene for a moment then say, "Frank, help me to help you. Let's be in the best position we can be in."

Let me remind you again that these are my words, my style. If they work for you, use them. If you like the idea but not the words or style, change them to fit you. This is true about everything I am sharing with you. There are a thousand different ways to say and do the same thing. Use what works for you. It's only words you already know. What you say and how you say it will have everything to do with the reaction you get.

Why Get the Down Payment with the Write-up

You might be wondering why it is important to get the down payment with the write-up. Why not wait until the deal is closed to get it. There are several good reasons not to wait. I am sure you will agree with them.

My #1 reason is not to firm up the deal. The reason is that it helps getting the salespeople comfortable asking for money. Once again, money is the only reason people do not buy what they want. Salespeople often have trouble dealing with money. Be it the price, down payment, or if need be to go back and negotiate for more money.

The down payment money is the easiest money to ask for. It is the money the customer wants and is willing to spend. If you are having trouble asking for the easy money then how much harder will it be to get additional money when it is needed?

By learning how to get the down payment at the time of the write-up you are also becoming a better closer. Remember. It is ONLY the down payment. It is not your money. If it is asked for simply, most of the time it will be simply given to you.

And yes, the deal just became stronger. When the customer writes the check or gives you a credit card or cash they are now so much more in the mindset of buying. Believe me. They don't want their money back. They want the motorcycle and you have now put them in a better position to be flexible if necessary to negotiate price, trade, down payment or payments.

Another reason is that you just made your sales manager more aggressive. When they are holding the money, they most certainly do not want to give it back. It is just logical that they now care more about the deal and just might think harder on how to put the deal together.

I hope these reason make it easy to understand that you, the customer, and the dealership are all in a much better position to close the deal if you get the down payment at the time of the offer. Everybody wins.

NOW WHENEVER I'M WITH a group of salespeople, I always ask where they think I can help them the most. The number one response is in helping them close more deals. "That's no problem." I always say, "Because it's a one-step procedure. Write up more customers."

The one who writes up the most customers will get the most deliveries. They'll also get the most turn-downs in financing and the most offers that can't be closed. More importantly, they will be the fastest to rise to the top.

More write-ups mean more of everything. The only way I know to increase volume is to increase the number of offers.

If you think about it, one of two things is going to happen with each customer. Either the customer is going to make you a committed offer to buy, or they're not. Later I'll deal with the ones who don't make you an offer. For now I want to talk about the attitude behind the write-up.

Think about a professional baseball player getting his shot in the major leagues after years in the minors. When he gets a shot in the big leagues he has a batting average of .200, which means he got just two hits out of every ten at bats. Not surprisingly, he won't last long. After about fifty at bats they'll send him back to the minors. He just couldn't make the team.

If a professional baseball player has a .300 batting average, or three hits for every ten at bats, he will stand a good chance of going to the All-Star Game and will probably make more than $5 million a year. Heck, he won't need the money he makes in baseball because McDonalds will pay him, Nike will want him, and the rest will be standing in line. He will be in demand.

So, what's the difference? One guy had an average of two hits for every ten at bats and he's traveling from city to city in the back of the team bus. The other batter had three hits for every ten at bats. He's a multi-millionaire flying on the team jet collecting endorsement fees on his way to the Hall of Fame. What's the difference? Just one extra hit out of every ten at bats.

Here's a question for you. Do you think the major leaguer who hit .300 only tried three times out of ten, or do you think he was focused on every pitch?

It works the same way in the sales game. To rise to the top by getting that one more sale out of ten isn't asking a lot, but it will change your life. I'll be asking a simple question at the end of this chapter, so remember the batting average story.

Your role on the team isn't to close or sell, not at first anyway. All championship teams are made up of players who know their job. Before a close or a delivery can take place, you must have an offer to buy. So concentrate on your role in the game plan, which is to figure out what it will take to get a committed offer from every customer. Once that is done *then* you can take your swings at closing if it's necessary.

It is very important to believe that the more offers you get from customers to buy the motorcycle of their dreams the more sales you will get and dreams you will fulfill.

Yes, you will also get more deals where the manager doesn't accept the offer from the customer or their credit was turned down. But you also will increase sales. It is a mathematical fact. More equals more.

Don't Fight It. Write it.

There are just two ways that a write-up can take place. One way is when the customer says, "Let's do it!" The other is when they make you an offer and you are wise enough to remember the rhyme, "Don't Fight it; Write it." Make sure this rhyme is a bullet in your holster, one you remember to use on a regular basis. Make it the foundation of your salesmanship.

The customer can say, "Let's do it!" in several different ways. The most common is just after you told them you have great financing and they show a real strong interest in the amount of the payments.

Remember, 80 % of buyers finance their purchase one way or another, so payments are their natural way of deciding if they will make a purchase.

Another way that happens is after you let them know about your great financing you follow up by saying something like, "If we could get you an affordable payment would you like to take it home with you today?"

In other words what you are saying is that you are willing to try whatever it takes to make the customer happy. You are their Help-You-Buy Person. So help them by using *all* of your game desire.

The customer can win or lose. They can win by being lucky enough to have you as their Help-You-Buy Person, or they can lose by buying somewhere else from someone else. If they do, they would lose out because they would not have you standing behind the product.

I feel this way because I know that no one else will give them the service after the sale that I will and I don't keep that secret. All I do is to tell them the truth about myself. I hope you feel the same way about yourself. If you do, please don't keep it a secret from your customers.

I believe that the service after the sale is just as, if not even more important than the deal itself. Once the deal is over, it is soon forgotten – but the service after the sale is ongoing. Done properly, many times it leads to a re-purchase and or referrals.

The - *If we could, would you?* Approach is an honest way of saying to the customer that we would love to have your business and are willing to do whatever it takes, within reason, to earn it. Remember, you can – "*If we could, would you*" to the point of being ridiculous. You're not saying you can get it. You're saying if they want to buy it, for whatever reason, you will try to get it for them. That's great. Now go try. Write it up and present it to the sales manager.

By doing this, most of the time you and the customer will be at least 90% of the way home. Sometimes the first commitment is at full price... or they might want a discount... or something thrown in with the deal... or whatever. They are allowed to ask and you are allowed to try. That's what being a Help-You-Buy Person is all about.

Of course if the customer gives you a price, you should not try to negotiate with them verbally. You should simply "Don't fight it, write it.

When a customer is sitting in your office waiting for you to give them your best price, I go to what I call the Cross-Cross method. I learned along the way that nothing matters if the customer isn't happy. If they are *unhappy* they aren't likely to be buying. If we make them *happy*, they will probably try to buy. So, then, what do we do? We try to make people happy. What a job. What a game. And we get paid for it!

When the retail price is still the issue, go ahead and write it where the price normally goes. Then explain to the customer this is the price most people buy at; but if they want to get a little better deal, you'd be happy to try for them. Then ask – as you run a couple of lines through the price (that's the Cross-Cross) – if they would buy at such-and-such price (you give them little bit lower price).

Here's an example of how this works:

` "Ron, really, seventy-five fifty is a super deal but what you're saying to me is if we could get you a better price, you would like to take it home with you today. Well, where would we be at (cross-cross) seventy-five even?"

Write it down as you say it, letting Frank see it as well.

If Ron says, "Yes" Great. Don't Fight it, Write it.

If he says it isn't low enough, ask him what is – but at the same time come down just a little bit more as you *cross-cross* seventy-five off, just as you did with the original price of seventy-five fifty.

Later, I'm going to do a complete write-up role play with Roger that should clear up any confusion you might be experiencing, but before moving on you must understand that you should always come down in small increments.

Consider this: If a customer has an idea of what they consider a good deal to be, they normally deduct some from that amount and make you an offer. They're just playing their version of the game. But if a customer doesn't think he knows what a good deal is, he will ask for your price and then probably make you a counter offer.

Two bad things take place if you drop a bunch off your initial price. First, the customer will think there is a lot of mark up in it. If you can come down so much, so fast, they could knock off a whole bunch, too. Second, the farther you go down the price hill the steeper the climb back up will be.

Half of deals that end up negotiated never need to be. It happened because the salesperson hit the zipper on the price quote when he was asked how much it was. It just makes no sense to do that. Do you think they would say, "Seventy-five fifty? That's too low. I'll only buy one today if you raise the price." I doubt it. The salesperson has forced the customer to say something like, "Can you do any better than that?" Now they just might have created the discount.

If you believe that a conversation starts where it was left off, and by now you should, what choice do you give a customer if you hit the zipper at seventy-five fifty?

By doing the switch-- The price is only seventy-five fifty, and we have the best financing in the world. Why don't we sit down and figure out some payment options-- You're getting your customers focused on the way they really buy: in payments.

What difference does the price make if the customer can't afford the payments? And from the other point of view, what difference should the price make if they can afford the payments?

There is no way I would check out million-dollar homes if I were looking for a place to rent. But if by accident I saw a million-dollar home in the classifieds for $500 a month, I'd jump all over it.

The payment is the big key that takes the pressure off your customers. Help them to make the easy decision of a small payment rather than a much harder decision of the total price. That's your role, being a Help-You-Buy Person. The $7,500 is rocks – A low monthly payment is feathers.

WHEN YOU GET A REQUESTED payment from a customer, you should write it on the write-up form. As you do, you should now ask the *"up to"* question. Here's an example:

"Brett, what payment was that you said you wanted?" I ask, unable to recall what he told me on the showroom floor.

"Around two hundred," Brett answers.

"That's right," I say as I write it down... "Up tooooo?" I ask as I slowly twirl my hands in a circle.

Brett responds quickly, "Oh, maybe two thirty."

"Two thirty," I repeat as I write it down, then say, "Great! But we will do our best to keep it closer to two hundred if we can."

Obviously the more flexibility you have to work with the easier it will be on everybody. If your finance department can get the lower payment, I am certain they will. But if they can't, you have made thirty dollars extra a month feel like feathers.

OKAY HERE IS THE question I promised I would ask at the end of this chapter. I want you to answer it honestly.

If you apply the things you liked about this book and went about it with a Gotta-Wanna attitude will you end up getting one more write-up out of ten customers you talk to?..........(Take a minute to think about it before you answer)..

If your answer is, "Yes!" I hope you know how much your life in sales will change. I promise your every-day life will change for the better too.

I told you the story about the difference of a baseball player's batting average. Hit .200 and he is back to the minors. Hit .300 and he is a millionaire. The difference is just one hit out of ten at bats.

Let's see how that kind of improvement would work for you. I will base it on the idea that you talk to 20 people a week and the understanding that 1 out of 2 write-ups turn into a delivery.

If you wrote up just one more out of ten then you would write up two more customers a week. If half of those turned into sold units then you will sell one more bike a week. You take two weeks off to go on vacation so you end up with 50 more sales a year....Hmm.

One out of ten is a huge difference isn't it? I will let you figure out how much that would benefit your life. You just gotta be one out of ten better to gain tremendous rewards. I hope I did my job and you believe that you are one out of ten better. If so, I really hope that you are smiling. I know that one more customer out of ten will be as they live the dream.

Chapter Eight
The Close

THE MOST IMPORTANT PART about closing a deal is the write-up. The most important aspect of the write-up is the probe. And the most important thing of all is the Gotta-Wanna. You put this package together and you have a guaranteed trip to the World Series of the sales game.

Consider this: When you need to close a deal, why are you doing it? Is it for the money? No doubt that's a good reason, but the money shows up last. It shows up after you close the deal—so it's a bad reason.

Believe me, I like to get paid too, but if the principal motive is the money, that's rocks. If you're showing an honest desire to come up with a compromise solution with the customer, that's feathers.

Feathers pay more and it is a lighter work load. I have a much more difficult time enjoying my day at the Bus Stop when I'm carrying a sack of rocks, but when I'm playing a game everything seems as light as a feather.

Remember, the name of the game is that everyone wins. A deal that needs to be closed after you have written it up is part of the puzzle game. Your game is Sherlock Holmes. If Sherlock Holmes can figure out how to put the pieces of the puzzle together, everybody wins. If he doesn't, everyone lost except you.

The company lost a sale and did not have a reduction in inventory. The customer left empty handed instead of with a fulfilled dream. As for you--you're a winner.

Winning or losing is not based on the children, that is, the results you have. It is based on the mother of them, your efforts. If you gave it your best-shot, if you went down swinging, you're still a winner. Good game plans and efforts breed better game plans and efforts and that produces future sales. There is nothing to gain or learn by not trying except to see the error of your ways.

That's what I mean about money being your motivator. If you're an all-about-the-money kind of salesperson, then you're a loser whenever you don't get the sale, and since you don't often get a sale, that kind of thinking makes you a loser almost every day. No one likes that. I know I don't. But if you're all about efforts, you can win every day.

Unlike the book character, a real-life Sherlock Holmes doesn't solve every single mystery. However he is focused on each individual case, gathering clues, then following them one step at a time in search of the missing piece that completes the puzzle.

The Help-You-Buy Sherlock Holmes goes down swinging because Sherlock Holmes is a winner. He is a winner because of his Gotta-Wanna attitude and his true desire to make the customer a winner.

WE WILL NOW WRITE-UP a customer I'll call Pam and see Sherlock Holmes in action. Once again, Roger Cooper is the lead character playing the part of Sherlock.

In 1975 my brother Ed took on the Honda car franchise. So I am going to make this a car story in order to switch it up a bit. Let me fill you in on a few things about Pam and Roger and what's happened up to this point.

Pam is in the market for a dependable used car as a surprise gift for her daughter on her sixteenth birthday at the end of the week. She has already gone to three other used car dealerships to see what was available.

One of the cars that she test drove appealed to her very much and she almost bought it but thought she should still look at a few more places. Besides, the salesperson didn't have much of a personality. Whenever he spoke, it seemed all he could say was how badly he needed to sell a car. When she told him she wanted to think about it, you could see the disappointment in his eyes as he grimly handed over his card. There wasn't an ounce of Sherlock Holmes in him.

Pam told Cooper about her visits to the other dealerships while they were out test-driving a four-year-old Toyota. She began opening up to Roger because of his questions and she shared all sorts of information about her daughter and two other younger children. She told him that she and her husband had twin boys soon to be fourteen. She half-smiled and half-grimaced as she mentioned they would also need cars in a couple of years.

The more she chatted with him like a friend would do, the more comfortable she felt. Soon Cooper knew what her husband did for a living and that he loved football (she didn't) and how old their dog was.

She also mentioned that she was splitting the car payment with their daughter and that she was planning to do the same with the boys once they were old enough to drive. She was hoping to find a reliable car and put down a thousand dollars and end up with payments around $200 a month.

When Pam and Cooper arrived back at the dealership, Cooper asked her how she felt about the car. Pam said she really liked it and that it was hard to choose between the Ford that she had driven at the other dealership and the Toyota that they had just test drove. Okay, you're caught up, now let's begin the role-play.

Pam: "I really liked it but I liked the Ford, too. Boy, making this kind of decision can be rough."

Cooper: "I know what you mean, Pam. But besides buying the car, whomever you get it from can make a big difference. I can't say anything about the other place since I don't really know them, but I do know us. We would love to have your business and I can promise you that I'll do all I can to keep you happy after the sale as I will while you're buying it. The way we look at it is if we make you happy when you buy here, and then keep you happy with our service after the sale, where will you buy your next car?"

Pam: "Right here of course."

Cooper: "And where would you send your friends?"

Pam: "I would send them to you, Roger."

Cooper: "Super, and that's what we do. We don't want just one purchase from you, Pam. We want all of the business from you and your family for many years to come. We know how important service after the sale is. Pam, is there anything we can do to earn your business today?"

Pam: "Well, I can tell you care more than the other guy. I tell you what, make me a good deal on the price and I'll buy it today."

Cooper: "That won't be a problem, Pam. Congratulations. Your daughter is about to get her first car and it is a really good one backed up by a great dealership."

Pam: "That sounds great. Make me a good deal."

Cooper: "Super, let's go to my desk and figure it out together." Roger starts walking toward his desk as Pam follows. They both sit down and Roger pulls out a write-up sheet.

Cooper: Now, Pam, I don't know if you're like me; but a good deal to me isn't so much the price as it is the payment. We have some super financing available and..."

Pam: "Financing is going to be important, Roger, but first make me a good deal on the price. That's what I'll base my decision on. When we were on the test ride you said the price is $9,995. How much better than that can you do?"

Cooper: "Okay, no problem, but before we make you happy on the price, let me explain a few things. It's the price where we can work with you. That is the part that is negotiable. There is also sales tax, license

78

fees, reconditioning and a couple of other minor charges that I can't do much about, but I know we can make you happy on the price. Pam, really, $9,995... (Roger says as he writes the number on his work sheet)... Pam, really $9,995 is a super deal on that car but where would we be at (cross-cross) $9,900 even?"

Pam: "Gee, Roger, that's only $95 dollars. You can do better than that can't you?"

Cooper: "Pam, I've found one thing out; It doesn't really matter what I think is a good deal. I'm not the one who is buying it. Besides, I think $9,900 is a good price, but you want a super price. So tell me. What's a super price, and I'll do my best to make you happy? Pam, how would you feel at (cross-cross) $9,850?"

Pam: "You're getting closer, Roger. Can you do any better than that?"

Cooper: "Pam, getting closer isn't going to help us. We need to know what it is we have to do to make you happy. Would (cross-cross) $9,800 do the trick?"

Pam: "Tell you what, Roger. If you can go $9,000, you've got yourself a deal."

Cooper: "$9,000 it is. Wow. That really would be a super price. Let me just write-up the offer and we will get the show on the road. Now as far as the down payment goes, the banks like, and most people like to put about a third down. That would be three thousand. Is that what you have in mind?"

Pam: "No, actually I'd like to put $1,000 down if I can. I'll write you a check."

Cooper: "Sure, that shouldn't be a problem. Like I said, we have some great finance resources. What payment was it you said you wanted?"

Pam: "$200 would work out perfect."

Cooper: "$200 up to-o-o-o-o"

Pam: "Oh, Maybe... maybe $230."

Copper: "Two-thirty, Super, but we'll do our best to keep it closer to two hundred. Okay, Pam, let me read to you what I'm going to take to my boss. We are looking at the blue Toyota four-door, stock # 319. Normally the price would be $9,995 but you want to get a super deal of $9,000 even. You want to put $1,000 down and finance the balance. You would like to get your payment between $200 and $230. Is that right?"

Pam: "Perfect. You get all that for me and we have a deal."

Cooper: "No problem. I just need you to okay the offer right here."

Pam: "What am I signing? This doesn't make me an owner does it? I still don't know what price I am getting it for.

Cooper: "No, Pam, this is just your offer. What you are doing is authorizing me to represent you. I'm about to go to my boss and talk about your money. You're giving me permission to do that. But let me ask you this, Pam, if my boss does say yes to this offer, we have a deal don't we?"

Pam: "Oh, I see. Yes. If they will go nine thousand I will buy it today."

Cooper: "Great, I just need your signature right here."

Pam: "Okay-dokey, let me borrow your pen."

Cooper: "While you got the pen, Pam, why don't you write out the down payment check and I'll take it in with the deal."

Pam: "No Problem, I can do that."

Cooper: "All right, shake my hand and wish me luck. I'm going to get you a super deal."

Pam: "Good luck, Roger. I'm counting on you to get me a good deal."

TIME OUT

What Cooper does now is go to his manager with the write-up. His manager does what managers do and gives a compromising counter offer of $9,880

TIME IN

Cooper: "All right, Pam. It worked. He came off of the price some and came up with a super deal. He came down to $9,880 and really that's a great deal on that car. (Switch) Why don't we look at the payments and see how they work for us?"

Pam: "No Roger. I mean, the payment does mean a lot to me but you've got to do better on the price or I'm going to go home and think about it."

Cooper: "Pam, we're too close to even think about quitting. How far apart are we? Let's see. You wanted $9,000 and my boss feels $9,880 is his best price, so we are only $880 apart. I really don't think you should let $880 stop you from getting the car you want."

Pam: "I don't know, Roger. Let me go home and talk to my husband and think about it for a day or so and I'll let you know."

Cooper: "Pam, don't give up. We're going to work this out. Now let's see, we're only $880 apart. Where would we be if we met in the middle and split the difference? Half of $880 is…$440 that would be a total price of $9,440. I think meeting half way is a fair offer. Don't you."

Pam: "Yeah, I guess it is. Okay, but that's it. If they don't take that, please bring my check back and I'll go home and think about it.'

TIME OUT

Cooper goes back to his manager and once again he gives Roger a counter offer. This time the manager splits the difference on them, leaving a balance of $9660. They are now still $220 apart.

TIME IN

Cooper: "Pam, you wouldn't let a two or three dollars stop you from buying the car would you?"

Pam: "No, not a couple of dollars. What price did you get?"

Cooper: "The boss came down to $9660. So the $220 difference in the price would make the payment *Only* a few dollars more. You should be able to take it home this afternoon."

Pam: "I couldn't pick it up until tomorrow when my husband gets off work. Is that really the best deal he can do?"

Cooper: "Really, Pam that is a super deal. And I promise when you see the joy on your daughter's face on her birthday and you have the peace of mind knowing she is in a dependable car, you're never going to think about the extra two or three dollars. Throw in the fact that if you ever need any help after you buy it, I'll show you the same effort to keep you happy as I did making your happy. My service comes at no extra charge.

Pam: "Your right. Let's go ahead and do it"

IT SURE IS EASY TO WIN when you make up a role-play. Then again, life is one big role-play, and you are the writer, star and director. So write that you win. Give a great and true performance and direct yourself to success. Lean how to improve it along the way by adding bullets that work and throwing out the blanks.

I could write a whole book on the write-up or the close, and I just might someday. There are so many different situations that take place and there's a way to handle each one of them. But you are the only difference that matters. A customer can usually find what you have in many places. They can get the same model, same year, and maybe even a lower price somewhere else. But price isn't everything that determines a good deal.

A good deal is one you feel good about. Feel good about yourself and your efforts. Feel good about who and what you represent. Give it your Gotta-Wanna and you're going to have a lot of good deals. Many times when you have all that going for you, there won't be much need for closing.

The Roll-Play You Just Read was just one example of

closing and negotiating a written-up deal. I hope you can read between the lines and see how much of this example applies to many other situations. If you take your game attitude and apply that same desire to win as you do when you're playing a regular game, you will be able to see the big difference it makes in your sales life.

The sales game is supposed to be fun. Many people wish they could have a fun job, but they're stuck. They never consider the sales game as a fun way to make a living. They don't understand that the fun isn't in the job—you bring the fun to the game with you. Selling gives you the freedom to do that. Be yourself, have fun, help people be happy, get paid. You call this a job? I call it a game

It's a little game inside the big game of your life. It's your Bus Stop. The best you can do at the Bus Stop is to enjoy your time—I believe that is the best any of us can do. Give me nothing but an enjoyable time any day over the wealth of kings who hate the time frame in which they are living. How much does it cost to enjoy the beauty of every day? About the same as it does to think and feel good?--Zero, no charge, yours for free.

Chapter Nine
The Wise Old Owl

I am now going to tell you a short cute story about a rabbit and a wise old owl. This story sums up the most important thing about reading this book.

The Wise Old Owl

There was a young rabbit that decided that there had to be more to life than just eating and lying around in the hole in the ground that he had dug. "I know what I will do," he said to himself one day. "I'll search for knowledge. Surely if I do find it, I'll have a much better life. I'll explore the woods and find out what there is to learn."

So the rabbit woke up early the next morning and began his search to obtain knowledge. Unfortunately for the rabbit there was a fox that lived in the woods. When the fox saw the rabbit he began chasing it. The young rabbit was faster than the fox and was able to escape back into the hole in the ground where he lived.

Day and night and night and day the same thing happened over and over again. The rabbit would begin his quest for knowledge just to have the fox chase him back into his hole. One day while the rabbit was contemplating his problem he came across the answer. The rabbit remembered there was a wise old owl that lived in a tree not far from him.

"That wise old owl knows everything," he thought. "Surely he'll know what I should do about the fox. I will tell him my situation and he'll give me the answer to solve it."

The next day the fox was nowhere to be seen which sometimes happened. The rabbit followed the trail that led to the tree where the wise old owl lived. When he arrived he called up to the owl. "Wise old owl, are you up there! Please come out, I have a big problem, I need your help."

From a hole in the top of the tree, suddenly appeared a gray old owl. "What is your concern rabbit? It better be important. You have awoken me from a deep sleep," the owl snipped and then yawned.

The rabbit said, "Wise old owl, I have a great desire to obtain knowledge and have a better life. But every time I go on a mission to find it I run into the same problem. You see, there is a fox that lives in the woods that would like to make me his dinner. He keeps chasing me back to my hole before I am able to learn anything. I know that you are the wisest of all creatures. Surely you can advise me as to what to do."

The wise old owl crossed his wings and then said, "Rabbit, the answer is simple. Just turn yourself into a tiger."

The rabbit thought about the owl's advice for a minute and then began to smile. "That's it, wise old owl!" the rabbit exclaimed. "That's the perfect answer. There's no way that fox will chase me around if I was a tiger." Then the rabbit asked, "How do I do that?"

The owl looked down at the rabbit and quickly responded. "Rabbit, it is my job to come up with the answer. It is your job to implement it."

Writing **This B**ook and Offering My Advice and you reading it is the easy part. In this case I am the wise old owl. In order for things to change in your life including your sales something about you must change.

Here is the point. Obviously you are searching for knowledge and understanding or you would not have read this book. But I am just one source. There are many other good books and tapes about sales and life to learn from.

Regardless of what you read, hear or see, it won't do any good if you do not turn yourself into the tiger of reason, understanding and, most important of all, *the tiger of implementing*. If I gave you some good ideas but you don't implement them, they were worthless. When you find an idea you like it will only be of value if you put it into motion in your thought pattern and actions.

Along your path you might come across different bummers and foxes that could change your direction and attitude if you allow it. Don't let them chase you back into the hole of sadness, depression or despair. Do whatever it takes to wipe them off and put them behind you.

It's your life, or as I would say your Bus Stop. They are your thoughts and inner feelings. They are your dreams, goals and desires. You are the captain of them. Nobody can tell you what to think or feel.

You are the writer, actor and director of your life. I hope you will write a great script. I hope you will act it out and win the Academy Award of life while playing the game. I hope you will direct your life and seek knowledge and understanding. Always remain the rabbit and learn all you can. This way you can also be the wise old owl when others need your help dealing with their foxes. Just remember to give your love freely and be extremely grateful for the love you receive.

Conclusion

So what has this book been about? What have I been hoping you would gain by reading it? First and foremost I will always believe that the winner is the buyer. You are getting paid for helping people to enjoy life more. You are not there trying to sell people something they don't want.

Understanding that people will buy from a friend, a lot more than they will from a salesman who is only about getting the sale. Creating a friendly relationship is the key to building sales. Not only ask questions about the motorcycle but also about the customer's everyday life. Be sure to listen to what they say. Everyone loves to be listened too. Many times customers will say important things that you can build the purchase around.

Remember that it is not your money being spent. It must be as easy to talk about as it is to talk about your favorite TV program. Always have the ONLY attitude when it comes to money.

The write-up is the winning formula to sales. You must believe that there is a way that all of your customers will buy. You must know that you can write-up any objection with the idea of "If we could solve that problem would you buy today?"

You must believe that the more write-ups you get the more customers you will make happy. You must believe that the more write-ups you get will mean more customers will be out riding their new motorcycle that they purchased from you.

Of course we want the purchase at full price, a large down payment, a long time job and excellent credit. But it doesn't always work that way. None of these things are required to get a write-up.

First get the commitment to buy before you get too involved in personal financial matters. If you do, you might hear something that makes you believe they can't buy so you don't write them up only to find out they purchased elsewhere.

Many customers that were turned down in financing the first time they tried to buy found a way to make the deal happen. Maybe the customer came up with more down payment money or got a co-signer. It could be several other reasons. If so they will remain loyal to you if you sincerely tried to help them the first time. And obviously if you don't write-up customers because you don't believe they can buy your write-up percentage will go down. And if the write-up percentage goes down you will sell less motorcycles.

It is easy to sit down the buyer, but you also want to do your best to sit everybody down. It is a great place to make sure you have answered every question. It is also a good time to remind the customer that you really want their business and will do all you can to make them happy when they buy. Also let them know that you will keep them happy with great service after the sale.

Remember to get their phone number and other contact information in order to inform them of up-coming events. You are now also in a position to stay in touch with them and keep the good personal relationship strong. Everybody likes to buy from a friend.

Think of everything good about your dealership. Think about all the things that are good about you. Think about the helpful information you know about the motorcycle. Think about all the ways your financing can make the purchase affordable. Now remember one simple thing. "Don't keep it a secret."

But most important of all I am hoping you bought into the Bus Stop theory and understand two things. Your customers have a limited time to enjoy their lives. When you ask them if a new motorcycle will make them happy and they say yes, then basically for the most part all you have to do is to make it affordable. If you do that then you have done a great thing and improved the quality of the customer's life.

But the Bus Stop theory is not just for the customers. It is for you too. Your time is limited as well. Don't waste it on things that can hold you back. A lot of people do. They focus on negative things and therefore are negative people.

Always remember how lucky you are. Right now you are reading this but many people can't because they are blind. Chances are you can walk, talk and hear; but many people can't. I could go on and on about things like that but I am sure you know what I mean. When something goes bad, always remember all the blessings you have. Let the good mean a lot more to you than the bad.

Understand that you cannot be the best salesperson you can be if you are not the best motivated and happy person you can be. And always remember that only you can tell you how to feel or what to think.

The End.....Sort of

Note

When I wrote my first book: You Gotta-Wanna: it was subtitled Life and Sales at the Bus Stop. I had so many awesome comments about the Life at the Bus Stop chapters that earlier this year I wrote another book called: <u>Life at the Bus Stop</u>.

If you found my outlook at life interesting and because it will cost me very little, I have added a few chapters of that book to the end of this one.

I will be telling a few of stories that I told in earlier chapters. But the stories are going to be told different than they were the first time. I expanded quite a bit on them.

If you do read the following chapters I sincerely hope they help you to have a better Bus Stop. But I also feel that the these chapters can help you to be a better salesperson because like I have said a few times already, you cannot be the best salesperson you can be if you are not the best motivated and happy person you can be. I do wish you tremendous success in both life and sales.

Chapter Ten
The Game of Life

Personally I Look at Life as if it was game with many seasons in it. I consider each day to be a game, every year a season. I like having this viewpoint because games are fun to play, and so should life be.

It's my Bus Stop, so I get to choose how I want to play each game. I have elected to have as much fun as I possibly can and play each game with a winning attitude. This is the best way I know of to create an enjoyable day at the Bus Stop and win as many games as possible. I use my game attitude when trying to accomplish the goals I have set for myself. The same holds true when I'm chasing my dreams and desires. I love to dream, and I hope you do too.

Football reminds me a lot of the game of life. In football, or more importantly your life, you should start each day with a game plan. You should set your goals for today's game and have a list of plays you want to run in order to accomplish them, keeping your desires on the end zone.

It could be a list of chores or a list of things you want to do. Maybe you want to work on your dreams. It might contain all three. Your strategy should be to play each game the best way you can. Always remember that nobody can stop you from trying your best except yourself.

Once you have outlined your game plan, you should remain focused on the plays that will lead you across the end zone. One preplanned step at a time, staying motivated and in motion.

Sometimes you will find that you need a breather, so you call timeout; that's understandable. There are timeouts in every game but I have noticed that often, people who are in the middle of their plans, become discouraged because they are behind in the game. Instead of staying motivated to catch up they decide to stop running their plays.

There is a price to pay for that reaction, like a longer list of things to do tomorrow shortening the time from the list of things they wanted to do. It might prevent them from working on their dreams, and that would be a shame.

I don't want to sound like I am tooting my own horn, but I believe that when I was a car salesman, I was one of the best in the world. But then again every good salesman believes that about themselves.

I can't say honestly that I was the best in the world but I can say that almost every month I won the bonus for being the top salesman at my brother's Honda car dealership. Out of the eight salespeople I worked with if I didn't come in first at the end of the month, then I was a close second. I never went more than one month without coming in first.

Contrary to all the salesman jokes you've heard, my success came from being fun, honest, sincere, and having a true desire to fulfill customer needs. This formula kept me on the top. That was until I let an uncanny circumstance send me reeling to the bottom of the pack for three consecutive months.

On one particular month the bonus for being top salesman was a thousand dollars. This was four times as much as normal and a lot more money than it is today. My brother needed to move inventory to make room for the next year's allocation so he increased the bonus to get the sales staff pumped up and that we were.

To understand how much money that was at the time, a thousand dollars covered three monthly payments for the house I was buying. I was looking forward to receiving it and taking my wife on a Hawaiian vacation. She naturally expected me to win it. She was so confident that she went to a travel agency and picked up brochures to the islands.

The race for first place was at a furious pace between Roger Cooper and me. Though we were the best of friends, we were also the fiercest of competitors. If I didn't win salesman of the month honors, he normally did.

That month we left the rest of the salesman in the dust. By mid-month it was obvious that either Roger or I was going to cash in. Back and forth Cooper and I went passing each other up on an every-other-day basis. Then on the first few days of the last week of the month I got hot and took a commanding lead. When the last day of the month was at hand I had four more sales than Roger with a couple of deals in the making. It looked like I had the prize locked up. I was counting the money. Then the unexpected happened.

An old Volkswagen van pulled into the parking-lot around noon. Roger went outside to do his normal, cheerful greeting. I couldn't believe my eyes one by one people started filing out of the van. There were a total of seven potential customers.

Five of the folks were family and the other two were good friends of theirs. Each one of them was looking for a new car and wanted a multi-purchase discount to earn their business. Obviously when seven people are going to buy they are entitled to a discount, and they got it.

Roger ended up selling seven cars in just a few hours and went zooming right past me and ultimately bagged the top salesman of the month award. Two of the deals I had working came through but he still beat me by a single sale. He won the thousand dollar bonus and I was crushed.

I was extremely depressed when I walked into my house that night, and my wife instantly knew something was wrong. When I told her how my bad luck day went, and that the Hawaiian trip wasn't going to happen, I could see the disappointment in her eyes. She was a trooper though, and she did her best to cheer me up, but I was not in the mood to feel good. I said I was tired and then went to bed sulking. All night long I tossed and turned as my stomach did. I kept thinking how I had blown a thousand dollar bonus and a fun trip for my wife and me.

The next day was the first day of the month. I was useless at work. I could not shake the feeling that I had lost and blamed it all on bad luck.

"Why didn't I greet the people in the Volkswagen van?" I kept asking myself. I was thinking why didn't one of the other salesmen get the deal? If they did I still would have come in first. Why did it have to be Roger? I lost my motivation to talk to people and spent most of the day just sitting in my office pouting.

The first day turned into a week. The week turned into two and the two weeks became a month. When it was all said and done I ended up in last place. From first to last, all because I couldn't shake one deal, one disappointment. My brother and sales manager did their best to motivate me and get me back on tract, but I wouldn't heed their advice. I was my own worst enemy and my pay that month suffered tremendously because of it. I became more depressed.

One of our duties as salesman was to make ten phone calls to customers a day. Some of the calls were to people who bought a car from us. The goal was to see if they were happy with their new car and if they had any questions. Then we would ask if they had any relatives or friends that they could refer to us.

We also made calls to customers who didn't buy the day they were in the dealership. We would call to see if there was anything we could do to earn their business in the near future. Another responsibility we all had to do was to send out thank-you cards to everybody we had talked to.

When I became de-motivated, the things that were previously easy to do became a chore to do. I would make one or two calls then send out less than half of the postcards that I was required to do. Soon I had a long list of calls to make and a nice size pile of cards to fill out and send. Because there was so much to do it slowed me down even more. I felt buried and was getting nothing done.

When the month was over and I was handed my check, it was less than minimum wage. In those days there was no guarantee. Whatever the commissions were on the cars you sold was what you got. No more, no less. Mine was way less than normal.

I felt sick when I saw it and knew I would have to get into my savings account to cover the bills. Problem was I had many material things that came with monthly payments and there wasn't much savings to draw from.

All of this depressed me even more and my attitude was worthless the following month and the month after that. Three bad checks in a row and I was broke. The savings account was depleted.
The stack of cards to send out and the list of calls to make had become what seemed like a mountain too high to climb. I was overwhelmed with duties to perform and was lost in the mess.

Understandably my brother and sales manager were very disappointed in me and justifiably on my case. I had come in last place that month and next to last the following month. Needless to say, I was pretty disappointed and perturbed at myself. I was honestly thinking about quitting and starting over at a competitor dealership. At least that way I could start fresh and not have so many lingering obligations.

I told Roger what I was thinking. His eyes widened and he shook his head, then he said with the utmost of sincerity:

"What? Are you nuts? Why would you even think about working for another dealership and compete against your own brother? You know more than I do that we have the best dealership in the state. Why are you letting one setback devastate you? Under your frustration still lies the best salesman I have ever worked with. I miss the old Steve who gave me a run for my money and I want him back. Your energy makes me push myself to keep up with you. Because your sales are down so are mine, you were my carrot. You set the pace. So here is the deal. You and I are going to dinner tonight to straighten it out."

His words struck a chord with me and I wanted to hear more of his views. He always could pump me up. So I agreed to meet him later at a buffet called The Kings Table which was across the street from the dealership.

After we filled our plates and sat down to eat Roger asked me why I had my head up my butt. I couldn't help but chuckle at his honest question. I knew he was right. Hearing it put that way made me smile and feel better.

"Coop," I said. "I was counting so much on the thousand dollar bonus. You heard me talk several times about the Hawaiian trip my wife and I were going to take. We had already talked to a travel agency and had the whole trip planned out. Because I got unlucky, and you sold seven cars at once I had to go home and break my wife's heart. I was crushed as well. I came so close to only end up blowing it. Now I am so far backwards on my follow up calls and cards to send out, I just can't get myself motivated to do them and it is so depressing. To top it off I have burned up all of my savings and I'm broke."

"Steve," Roger said sincerely. "Why do you feel it was your bad luck? Why not think of it as my good luck besides it really isn't luck. I got to work early and gave it my best shot. I deserve to have good things happen. You had many good things happen to you this year. Why not concentrate on them and wipe off what happened three months ago. You've lost way more than a thousand dollars not being able to move forward. Think of all the lost commissions. You know the best way to build your savings back up is to be at the top of your game. Only you can make that happen."

I knew Roger was right. I'd let not winning a thousand dollars cost me over five thousand in commissions. I had let the dragon of despair take over my thinking and being. I began to see the light and the wisdom in his reasoning.

Roger did work hard and he'd stayed close to me in the race. I had good fortune in the beginning of the month to take the lead over him. It wasn't just the seven car deal that caused him to win. It was all of his efforts combined that produced a winner. I realized how much of a baby I'd been. I knew it was time to shake it off and get back into the game. But I still had a heavy burden of the work that I let pile up and I whined to him about it. Then Roger brightened up my day even more.

"I tell you what Steve, I'll come in tomorrow on my day off and fill out your cards while you make your phone calls. If we take them one at a time before you know it you'll be caught up. Don't focus on all of them just think about the one you are working on." I gratefully accepted his offer.

Roger showed up first thing in the morning with his normal cheerful attitude. Even though it was his day off and his only purpose to be there was to help me, he came in pumped up as if he was doing it for himself. He filled out every card while I made my calls. I finished seventy-five percent of them that day in between talking to customers. Over the next couple of days I was caught up.

I was genuinely appreciative of Roger's help; not just in filling out cards but how he transformed my attitude. I knew how blessed I was to have a friend like him. Our friendship worked both ways. There were times Roger needed a kick start. I am proud to say I was there for him as he was for me. I must admit it was not hard to help my good friend in his time of need. I knew he would obviously do the same for me.

I gave it my best shot that month to win top salesman, but I came in second. Roger beat me by a couple of deals. When he got his bonus check I sincerely congratulated him and then said it will never happen again. Roger smiled and said, "Bring it on." The following two months I was back on top. I had learned my lesson and put it to good use I became a better salesman and person because of it.

Shortly thereafter Roger and I were promoted to managers. I became the sales manager when Mr. Bloomer left and took a different job. Roger became the used car manager. We were a great team. We had grown and now had a sales crew of sixteen salesmen. We did a super job at keeping the sales team motivated at doing their best. We smoked our competition and I will always believe it was because of Roger and me. Our attitude rubbed off on the sales staff and we just out performed the other dealerships.

I learned many things from my down experience that have helped me tremendously over my lifetime. One of them was to never let the list of things to do pile up. It will not only bog you down but it can leave you standing in place. The end result will be that the work load will only be heavier, making it even more depressing.

But the biggest lesson I learned was to look at life as if it were a football game. Just like in football, life has a defense that will block or change your path. I'm talking about the unexpected bummers of life. When they show up they can cause you to be slowed down or push you away from the direction you've planned. I wish that wouldn't happen, but it does. When this does happen to you, it is then time to become the coach of the game and re-write the plays you are going to run.

An unexpected bummer is like a lost fumble. When that happens, you are now on defense. Your job is to tackle the bummer until you get the ball back. If you do that with a good game attitude you will find that you will get the ball back sooner than later. The sooner you have the ball, the sooner you can score. It should be easy to understand that the better attitude you have while being on defense, the more games you will win.

One of my ways of scoring is when I cross something off the list that I prepared the night before. At night I almost always write down the things I want to accomplish the next day.

Often at the end of my day, I end up with a few things crossed off the list that were not on my list when I started the day. I was not able to run the plays I intended because of the defense of distractions and bummers. If I crossed off everything I possibly could, with a good attitude, I still won the game. But like the saying goes, you can't win them all though you can always try your best.

Another way to look at unexpected bummers is to think of them as the *penalty flags of life*. Some of the penalty flags are deserved. We got penalized because we took ourselves out of game and stopped running our plays. We became side tracked, sad or depressed and we stopped playing. Unfortunately, the list of things is still there and probably growing, but the amount of time on the clock is now shorter.

Hopefully if this happens in your game, you will accept the flag you deserved and the yardage lost. It is okay to moan and groan for a few seconds when the flag is thrown, but don't let the dragon burn inside you, not for long anyway.

When I lost the one thousand dollar bonus on the last day of the month that was not the penalty flag. That was just the game. I threw my own penalty flag deflating my attitude. You can't win them all no matter how much you want to, or how hard you try.

Sometimes you come so close to your goal and still lose by one point. It hurts when that happens, but it does happen. What I did was throw my own flag against myself. I took myself out of the game. When the final score was announced, I started sitting on the sidelines, how stupid.

Because I'd benched myself I lost a lot more than I needed too. I should have just accepted the score and played to win the next game instead of sulking about the loss. I deserved the results of my self-inflicted penalty and it took me three unnecessary months to understand what I did and learn from it. And learn I did.

The best thing to do when you have a setback is to coach yourself to get back into the game as soon as possible. Penalties happen, we all make mistakes, we all step out of bounds. The key is to learn and not make a habit out of our mistakes.

There's no denying that some of the penalty flags we get are undeserved. Even if we didn't deserve it, the flag was thrown just the same, and we still have to pay. We lose yardage. We are forced to put our plays on hold.

When this happens hopefully you will accept the penalty, leaving the dragon out of the equation, resolve the situation, and then continuing to play the game, focusing on the next play, instead of the penalty flag.

I have had many penalty flags in my life that I did not deserve. The one that sticks out in my mind happened when I was in fifth grade. I was as innocent as can be but the penalty flag was still thrown and I had to pay the price.

An un-just penalty flag

My 5th grade teacher said something to the class that made us all very excited. She said that because we had been so good during the day, she was going to give us an extra 15 minute recess. "Yahoo!" I yelled out loud. This was great news to me and it made my game day seem a whole lot better.

I loved playing catch. So when I got outside I found a friend and we started throwing a ball back and forth to each other. Sometimes we'd toss grounders or sometimes pop flies. We were doing this while standing next to the bicycle rack, which was full of bicycles.

While we were playing, a couple of other kids decided to hop on a bike and start riding them around. I knew this was not good as we were told more than once that we were not allowed to ride our bikes during the school day. Besides that, the bikes they were riding, were not theirs.

I said to them, "Come on guys, put the bikes back or we'll never get another extra recess again." They ignored my plea and continued riding the bikes.

Another classmate saw what the other two boys were doing and decided to join them. He picked out a bike and began riding it. The problem was when he peddled away he bumped another bike and knocked it over. I saw what he did and thought, "What a jerk." I stopped playing catch and went over to the bike and picked it up to set it back in the rack.

Unfortunately for me, right when I was doing that, the principal came out and told the three boys that were riding the bikes to go to the office. He glanced over at me and saw the bicycle in my hands. He assumed my intention was to ride it, so he told me to go to the office too. I obeyed his command and innocently marched my way there. I was positive that once I explained the situation he would say I did the right thing and to go back outside and play, maybe even say he was proud of me.

When we were all in his office he gave us a lecture about life and its responsibilities. I tried to explain my circumstance but he told me not to interrupt. Then he told us to get in a straight line and bend over. He was holding a paddle in his hand. I was first in line and before I could say another word, SMACK, the penalty flag that I did not deserve was thrown.

When the other three kids saw what happened to me, they began to sob and cry. It did no good. They still got the penalty, only they deserved it. I remember being very proud of myself because I kept my composure and did not join in the chorus tears. I quivered a bit but I did not cry.

The principal then gave us another penalty. Just like Tom Sawyer we were ordered to white wash the fence that surrounded the bicycle rack area. We were each allocated our own individual portion of the fence to paint. We had to do it after we ate our lunch. We were not allowed to play with our friends until the chore was finished.

During class that day I thought about telling the teacher my side of the story, but I reasoned that the teacher would probably not believe me and it would do no good. Besides, white washing a fence to this 5th grader sounded intriguing. In a weird way I was looking forward to doing it.

The next day after I finished my lunch I tackled the job with vigor and energy. The other kids took their time to begin their chore. Once they did, they moped around and complained between strokes. Because of my attitude I finished my portion that day. The others had to use two lunch breaks to complete theirs.

I've told this story many times to friends and family members. At the end of it we would laugh. Normally the people I told it to would say that it reminded them of a time in their life that they got a penalty flag they did not deserve. Almost every time after hearing about it we would have a good chuckle. Most of the time they would tell me that something good came because of it.

When I was in 5th grade I was too young to realize the valuable lessons I learned from that incident. As I grew up and learned to tame the dragon I reflected back to those days. What I learned helped me to get through many penalty flag situations. If I deserved the flag, I thought about the boys who were guilty of the deed. They did not man-up to what they did. They pouted and whined causing them to take twice as long to resolve the matter. They also had a lot less fun doing it as I did.

If I didn't deserve the flag but still received the penalty, I accept it for what it is. I then concentrate on the solution if there is one. If there isn't, I say," Bummer" and then wipe if off of my mind. I do not let it affect or side track me from running the next play. Attitude is the key to a winning day. I own it outright. It is always at my command.

Think about what the other choice is. Have you ever watched a sporting event where a player argues too strongly that the penalty flag was not deserved, and then he got thrown out of the game? It happens a lot in life too. Milk does get spilled. It does no good crying about it. When it happens, you will have to change the play you were running.

The same thinking holds true to all the other circumstances that force us to side step our game plan. When life throws you a penalty flag, deserved or not, you will have one of two choices to make. You can choose to suffer, get depressed, but you still have to deal with the consequences of the flag.

You can let the dragon burn inside by feeding him the negative attitude fuel it takes in order for him to breathe his fire. You do this by staying focused on the flag instead of figuring out what the next play is. Eventually you'll get through it and move on. Just like you did, with all of the other flags that now are in your past. It's just a matter of how much time you let it keep you out of the game before you allow it to become a cartoon you didn't get to finish.

Think of a penalty flag that you were once upset over but now is buried in your past. If it was burning you on the inside at the time and it held you back, ask yourself why? Try to remember what was so important that the stress and pain were worth it. More than likely you'll say it wasn't. You will probably agree that it is now just a cartoon that you didn't get to finish. Don't you wish now you would have just said bummer and moved on without experiencing the fire?

Know you could have, if you wanted to. It is very important to believe that. If you don't, how can you do it now?

Chapter Eleven
The Bummers of Life

It's a Beautiful Day. The sun is shining bright. There is a cool breeze that takes the edge off the heat. You could not have picked a better day to go for a walk. You're thinking of how good everything has been in your life lately and feeling extremely appreciative of it. Then all of a sudden you feel that all too familiar squishy, slippery feeling under your foot. AHHH, dog poop. Bummer! I hate it when that happens, especially when you don't discover it until you're driving the car.

To me the word 'bummer' is a good way to describe a situation you wish had never happened, but oh well, you can live with it. You moan and groan a bit when you realize what you stepped in and then move forward.

Now I do understand that if your head caught on fire you probably wouldn't say, "Bummer, my head's on fire." I'm sure you would come up with more animated words to express your feelings, and at times I do too. But most of life's downers really are just bummers. I am convinced that dogs were created to teach us how to wipe off the other bummers of life.

Have you ever been out walking with a good friend, having an enjoyable conversation, when squish, they step in it. They start moaning and groaning and using language like you have never heard them use before. What are *you* doing? Chances are you're laughing your butt off.

Here's my point: I am trying to learn to laugh it off when bummers happen to me. If I do, then I will discover the art of removing myself from the darkness of depression when dealing with unpleasant situations. Chances are I would tell the next friend I ran into what I stepped in and have a good laugh. Many bummers are funny stories later. The trick is to see the humor at the time or at least as soon as possible.

If only we would learn how to follow the same principle when we experience life's other problems. Bummers are part of the game. There is nothing I can say that will make it so we never have them, but how we decide to handle them is what I am talking about.

The best we can get at the Bus Stop is a long wait until the Bus arrives. The irony is that the longer the wait, the more bummers we have to experience. Those are the rules to the game. You can cry and suffer over them as long as you want, but you will still have to handle your problems one way or another. Hopefully somewhere along the way you will realize that all problems eventually become nothing more than a cartoon you didn't get to finish. Oh well, bummer.

To prove this point, go to a graveyard sometime. I suggest you wait until there are no living people around and then yell out, "Hey everybody, your car payment is really late! Your rent is way overdue." Not one person whose Bus showed up is going to care. Nope, not one little bit,

We have heard many times that we can't take our money with us. They should always mention that we also will not be taking our problems with us. Everything is a temporary situation including our problems. To let them ruin your day is far worse than the actual problem, because soon enough you will get over the problem, but you can never replace the day.

If you have a problem that you let stress and depress you, well, now you have three problems. I know people, and you probably do too, that because of a temporary situation, became stressed and depressed, and stayed home from work for a couple of days. Because they did that, their paycheck didn't cover the bills. Now they have a lot more problems. Then they become more stressed and depressed. Back and forth they go, dancing with the dragon.

Down the road I bet they wished they'd said, "Bummer," then focused on whatever it took to wipe it off. That's one cartoon down. That beats the heck out of dealing with the other problems that they created by focusing on the pain of the problem instead of the solution.

If we would just say, "Bummer" when the first problem happens, realizing soon enough it would become a cartoon we didn't get to finish, then all we would have had to deal with was only one problem. And sometimes there is nothing we can do about the first problem. Bummer.

Thieves can break into our homes and steal everything we own. Things get broken. Our car could get totaled. Death of friends and loved ones and some destruction are certain if we have a long wait at the Bus Stop. There are going to be some things in life that we can do nothing about other than to except them...Bummer...and move on.

But nobody can take or steal our attitudes and the way we're going to think and feel. It's all within our control. We are the writers, director, and stars of all our inner feelings and desires. I suggest that you write a good script then act it out. Direct your path and create the star you deserve to be. You can do it. I know that everyone can if they want to.

How we internally deal with bad or sad situations has always been in our control. It just depends how good of an actor you are. Because even if you are acting as if it was nothing more than a bummer and wipe it off and move on, soon enough, like so many other bummers in your past, you won't remember or care about it in the near future.

It's bad enough to experience the problem, why pay the price twice, by letting it reach the dragon of depression? Many times the second price will cost a lot more than the original one. The worst part is that you would be the one who charged yourself, by feeding the inner dragon. Do you know what I mean?

To me the inner dragon was a burning tormenting ugly feeling in the pit of my stomach consuming me with negative thoughts. But I learned it didn't have to be that way and I became a dragon tamer. I also learned that many times I could have avoided a bummer if I would have had a little bit better game plan.

Let's say you are driving home after a hard day at work. You were so busy that you didn't have time for lunch. You just can't wait to get home and eat dinner. About three miles from pulling into your driveway you hear a sound that reminds you of a firecracker going off. You instantly know that the back left tire has just blown out. Bummer, now you have to change it. This upsets you. You wish you didn't have to deal with it right now, but you have to, so you do.

105

As you get out of the car, you begin mumbling to yourself about how much this sucks. As you pass by the flat tire on your way to the trunk, you call it a few choice words then give it a hard kick to show your displeasure. Ouch that hurt!

As you open the trunk, you cannot believe your eyes. The spare tire is flat also. You kept meaning to get it fixed but just never got around to it. "Damn!" you scream and punch the trunk after you closed it. Ouch that hurt.

As you begin limping home, holding your sore hand, you start thinking how terrible your luck has become. You're trying to figure out why this is happening to you? You weren't bothering anybody. You worked hard today, giving it all you had. Even though you had to work through lunch, you still kept up a good attitude. "So why is this happening," you wonder out loud. You begin to shake your head because the only answer you get is that it starts raining… really hard.

Finally your house is in sight. You decide to cut across the lawn instead of going up the walkway. Squish, you guessed it. "Why me," you begin to sob as you wipe the bottom of your shoe on the lawn, but not good enough.

The second you walk in the door, you can feel the heat inside of the house. Awe, it feels so good, but not as good as the smell of dinner in the air. Man, are you hungry.

As your wife notices you standing there, dripping water on the carpet that she just vacuumed, she begins shouting at you about the stuff you are smearing into the rug.

"That's it!" You say to yourself. There was no, "Hello honey, Why are you all wet? And why are you limping and is that blood on your hand?" No, it was just nic- nic- nic- bla- bla- bla. So you blow up with the anger that was created by a flat tire instead of focusing on repairing it.

Well, because of the belligerent way you explained yourself at an extremely high volume, you ended up without dinner because it just landed in the garbage followed by the sound of a slammed, locked, bedroom door.

As you look out the kitchen window, you notice both of your garbage cans are full. Oh no, today is Wednesday. The garbage man comes on Wednesdays. The doggone kids forgot to take the cans out to the road, again.

"Kids!" you yell out. "Come here right now!" You begin shouting at them without even giving them a chance to explain anything to you. You know how kids are; they can always come up with a bad excuse as to why they didn't do what they were supposed to do.

You ended up yelling at them so much, that you made them cry. When you are done with the lecture, you send them to bed without supper. You had to because supper was in the garbage. Ouch that hurts.

As the children run crying to their room, the good ol' family dog comes running up, excited to see you. He's wagging his tail, staring at you with his loving eyes. You look down on his panting face and then remember what you stepped in while crossing the lawn. With one quick kick of your soiled shoe, you give your dog a flying lesson.

You just woke up with a darn kink in your neck. Seems like every time you sleep on the couch this happens. You glance at the television that you left on and hear the announcer say, "Have a very pleasant Wednesday morning."

Wait a minute you say to yourself, if this is Wednesday morning then *today* is garbage day! Not yesterday. You just realized why the children were trying so hard to explain why they didn't take the garbage out. Ouch that hurts.

You repair the tire then go to work. The bouquet of flowers you sent your wife, along with a card, that invited her out to a fancy dinner, worked. She called you to say that they were beautiful and that she forgave you. You then gave her the good news. The doctor said that the x-ray revealed that there were no broken bones in your swollen hand. She then informed you that because the two of you were going out to such a nice dinner, she would need to get her hair done. She would also need to buy a new dress of course, along with a pair of matching shoes.

Just before she hung up she told you that the kids send their love. She said that they can't wait to get the new bicycles you promised them for being a butt-head.

You told her you would take care of everything as soon as you got home from work. You reminded her that you would be a little late because you first had to stop by the veterinarian's office to pick up the dog.

A month or so later you're sitting at your desk looking over your credit card statement. Let's see there is a $59.95 charge for the flowers. Dinner with the tip was $136.00. Hairdo ran $65.00. Dress and shoes along with the belt and perfume she just had to have, totaled $292.00. The bicycles cost a total of $345.00. The x-ray and pain pills ran $160.00 and the vet bill was $89.50. This equals a grand total of $1,147.45. Ouch that hurts. Oh yeah, I forgot to add the $10.00 to fix the flat tire.

Okay, I agree, this is an off-the-wall story but I am sure you get the point. Tires are going to go flat. Other bummers in life will come and go. Cry and stress out and kick the dog if that is what you want to do. It's your Bus Stop. It's your call. Just know that it is a decision that you are willingly making by staying focused on the dragon. Just be prepared to pay the additional costs. I for one have elected to say bummer and concentrate on what it will take to fix the tire and move on. Total cost was $10.00 and I tamed the dragon.

We can't do much about tires going flat or any of the other bummers that happen, but we can do everything about how we handle them. Do you honestly believe that in six years and two months you will remember changing a tire? Sure, it was a bummer at the time, but even if you do remember, you certainly won't care.

You lived all your life until then not thinking about that tire. After you fix it, you won't give it another thought until it happens again. Then what? Chances are you will handle it in the same way you did the last time. Hopefully you did it with a good Bus Stop attitude. If you didn't do it then, that's okay. Just do it from now on.

Think of bummers you've experienced in the past. How did you handle them? Have you let one bummer cause others? If you have, turn it into a good thing. You are now in a position to learn from your mistakes. Of course, learning is one thing and applying what we've learned is another. If you do both, you will have a much better time at the Bus Stop.

Just like in the flat tire story, many times we could avoid having to deal with additional problems if we would direct our lives a bit more effectively. If we'd fixed the spare as soon as we knew it was flat, instead of putting it off, we would have ended up just changing the tire and paying $10 to repair the tire.

It's one thing if you didn't know it was flat. It's another thing if you did. What were you waiting for? A flat tire? You know the rules to having a car. Tires go flat... Bummer. (I hope you know I am not just talking about tires.)

Be prepared whenever possible. By doing this many times you will end up with a $10.00 bill instead of $1,147.45 credit card statement.

I used a flat tire in my story but I am confident that you realize the tire represents many other bummers that come our way in life. The spare tire represents being prepared for the unexpected. And always remember you can whistle while you work. You can feel good even when things go bad.

I had a bummer happen to me when I was in 6th grade that I will never forget.

King of Bonney Lake

I went to a small town elementary school in Bonney Lake, Washington. When I was in 6th grade there was a 5th grade girl by the name of Connie Tidball who was the younger sister of a good friend of mine. She had a crush on me but my 6th grade heart belonged to another.

Every year the 5th and 6th grade class would vote for a girl and boy 6th grader to be the king and queen of the school. The winners of the vote would get to ride in a convertible in the local Daffodil Parade and wave at the spectators.

I would have to say that I was the second most popular kid in class. Rory Turner was a notch ahead of me. I totally expected him to win. What I didn't know at the time was Connie had convinced the 5th grade class to vote for me. The 5th graders had a bigger size class than the 6th grade did.

When the voice came over the intercom and announced that I was the king I about fell out of my chair. "Wow!" I thought, I couldn't believe that I was the king. The best part of the amazing news was that Saundra Hill was elected queen.

Saundra had all of my young heart. Saundra was so everything to me. She made my head go light and made my legs wobble. Problem was, Saundra couldn't stand me. Well, that's what I thought at the time. Later on in life at our ten year high school reunion she confessed that she liked me as well but in 6th grade she felt she had to act like she didn't.

How she felt at the time didn't matter to me. All that mattered to me was that I was the king and she was the queen. We would be spending the following Saturday sitting next to each other while riding in the parade.

I grew up poor. Saundra lived in a big house on the lake. At the time I felt anyone who had a house on the lake had to be extremely rich. I was humbled by this feeling so I hatched up a plan to impress her.

I went house to house knocking on doors collecting empty pop bottles. At the time there was a two-cent refundable deposit on them. When I accumulated 50 of them I turned them in at the local store. I took my reward in the form of a one dollar bill.

Finally the big day came. There I was sitting next to Saundra, I was in heaven. I would occasionally rub my arm up against hers sending shivers down my spine.

I had put the one dollar bill in my shirt pocket with the end of it sticking out so Saundra could see that I was a man of wealth. There I was riding down Main Street with my beloved.

While waving at the people I would check to make sure the dollar bill was visible. YIKES! It was gone. It had somehow fallen out of my pocket and was now blowing in the wind. I had lost my fortune.

"Oh, darn," I said out loud when I realized what had happened. Saundra turned towards me and asked me what was wrong?

I knew this was the moment of truth. If I sniveled about the money she would know how important it was to me. I didn't want her to think that was all the money I had. So I said very nonchalantly that I had lost a dollar but it was no big deal and somehow brought myself to smile and continue waving.

There was a smile on the outside of my face, but the dragon was burning deep within me. My special day was ruined. I had it worked out so perfectly but life had foiled my plans.

At the end of the parade all of the kings and queens were given an ice cream. I thought to myself, "You know, ice creams are twenty-five cents apiece. I would have bought one for myself and been more than happy to buy one for Saundra. That would have cost me fifty cents," so I felt fifty percent better.

My whole inner attitude was changed by my reasoning. Soon I felt a hundred percent better and totally enjoyed my final moments with Saundra. I was so grateful that I had figured out the ice cream scenario because it dowsed the flame of the dragon.

I have thought about this story many times throughout the course of my life. Whenever a bummer takes place I think of what I have to be grateful for. I have family, friends, air, food, water, the mountains, the ocean, and many other blessings.

No matter what has taken place in my life I have figured out that I had more than 50% of good things to concentrate on. This does not make the bummer go away but it does make it easier to deal with and helps to leave the dragon out of the equation.

I feel I have gained millions of dollars in inner peace by the loss of one single dollar. I learned at a very young age *that what you think is how you will feel.* But to be honest, it did take me awhile to apply it.

We all had great grandfathers who had great grandfathers who had great grandfathers and so on and so on. Every one of them were dropped off at the Bus Stop and eventually picked back up. Each one of them had bummers in their life, yet today nobody cares. Most importantly neither do they.

You will have great grandchildren who will have great grandchildren who will have great grandchildren. How much will they care about your bummers? Most importantly, how much do you think you will care? I think you'll agree that those bummers will be less than a cartoon you didn't get to finish.

To realize this before the Bus comes is the key to a contented life. Nobody has to give you any advice when it is a sunny day and everything is going good. This is a great time to remind yourself of the problems you don't have anymore; the ones that you solved and wiped off. By realizing this, you can tell yourself, when you are dealing with a new bummer, that it too will pass.

You should realize that sooner or later you are going to step in another pile. Bummer... But now you know it doesn't have to stink. You can possess this kind of attitude if you want to because it's free to own.

I do understand that sometimes we do need to pull ourselves out of the game and take a time out. There is a season for all things and sometimes there will be a season of sorrow. When that season appears, then take the time you need to morn whatever it is that you lost. I hope you do not go into overtime of your sorrow. Be your best friend and pick yourself up and get back into the game of life as soon as possible.

Chapter Twelve
Ouch That Hurts

Several Times In the previous pages I threw in the comment "Ouch that hurts." Did you notice when I did that? All of them came as result of a self-inflicted wound.

I have been guilty of doing this and have seen several other people do it more than once. Because of a temporary unpleasant event they became upset. Because they are focusing on the problem, instead of the solution, they do things like punching a hole in the wall. Sometimes they kick or throw things. Worse yet I have seen them yell and scream at loved ones. I have witnessed people lose friends, jobs and end good relationships because they could not control their inner frustrations that in time would have just faded away.

They do this because they are feeling the dragon's breath, breathing its fire, in the pit of their being. They still end up with the original situation that was upsetting them. Only now they have other self-inflicted burns.

It could be a hole in the wall or a sore hand. It might be broken things that will need to be replaced. Worse yet, the people you really love are now upset with you because you said or did things that you did not mean to say or to do.

The burning negative fire can cause us to act or speak out of control. Then after we do get our composure back and reflect on what we said or did, we end up saying, "Ouch that hurts!" Then we have to spend the time, energy, money or make apologies to repair the damage we caused. This doesn't have to happen if you have learned how to tame the dragon.

Punching a hole in the wall is not the problem. It is the result of the internal fire within them. The heat was burning deep inside of them until finally they released their energy in a very negative way. The main problem isn't the one that is upsetting them. The main problem is that they are upset. The reason they are upset is that they are focusing on the bummer of the situation, instead of the solution, which in turn caused them to lash out.

Self-inflicted bummers can end up costing them more than the original one did. I had a friend I used to work with by the name of Kevin. We were both salesmen at my brother's Honda car dealership. He was a really nice guy most of the time but he did have a problem with his temper when he got agitated.

The first thing we were supposed to do when the morning shift began was to unlock the cars that were on the front line. One morning I was unlocking the cars with another salesman by the name of Gary. Kevin was nowhere to be found. I was a bit perturbed that Kevin was not there to help us as it was a very cold and icy Oregon winter's day.

About a half an hour after Gary and I unlocked the cars, Kevin walked in the building shivering and shaking. His face was beet red. It was easy to tell he was not happy, and I could understand why when he told us his story.

Kevin started at the beginning which began the night before. He said on the way home last night he was going to get gas for his car, but he was running late because he really wanted to watch Monday Night Football as his favorite team was playing, he decided he would fill up his car in the morning. Problem was he forgot to do it and ran out of gas on the drive into work and had to walk over a mile in the freezing cold to the dealership.

I could tell Kevin was furious at his mistake and was burning on the inside. All morning he kept murmuring to himself and you could easily tell he was really upset.

Kevin and I took our lunch break together so we could solve his problem. We went to our service department and got a gas can and filled it up with gas. I then took him to his car which was parked on the side of the road. After we put the gas in the tank Kevin was still very upset. He jumped in his car and peeled off spraying gravel all over my car which was a dealership demo. One of the flying debris hit the windshield and put a nice size chip in it. Now Kevin would be responsible to pay for the damage.

On my return to the dealership I watched Kevin speed through a stop light that was more red than yellow. I waited at the light until it turned green and then continued on. As I drove down the road I began to shake my head at what I saw next. There was Kevin parked back on the side of the road with a police car behind him with his flashing lights on. The officer was talking to Kevin through the driver's side window. It didn't look good.

Kevin arrived at the dealership about fifteen minutes after I did. When he walked inside he was holding a green slip in his hand and had a fearful scowl on his face. When I greeted him, he grunted out a handful of choice words then ripped the ticket in half, flung it in the air and stomped off to the rest room. I picked the two pieces of paper off the floor and put them in my pocket and figured I would give them back to him once he calmed down.

An hour or so later, Kevin went on a test drive with a customer. When they pulled back into the lot Kevin and his customer got out of the car. I could see through the showroom window they were arguing.

Our sales manager at the time was Mr. Bloomer. He had trained both Kevin and me. Nothing in his teachings ever hinted that there should ever be a disagreement with the customer. On the contrary, we were taught to always be respectful and courteous, not only to our customers but to every employee as well.

Mr. Bloomer noticed what was going on from his upstairs office and briskly marched downstairs and outside to see what the problem was; ten minutes later he was back inside. Yet, the customer and Kevin had driven off in separate cars. I asked Mr. Bloomer what happened.

He told me that Kevin was pushing the customer to get his car appraised in order to trade it in. The customer wanted to come back another time after he test drove a few different cars at other dealerships. Kevin took offense to his request and got upset that the customer was wasting his time.

I had got to know Kevin pretty well over the time we worked together and I knew this was not his every day style. He normally was quite pleasant and well-liked by his customers. He was just having a really bad day and was experiencing a meltdown.

I asked Mr. Bloomer where Kevin went. He told me that he tried his best to calm Kevin down so he wouldn't lose his job. He said Kevin threw the F-bomb at him a few times and told him to stick the job where the sun never shines and then said he quit.

I was saddened by this news as I knew how much Kevin enjoyed working there. But after Mr. Bloomer told me what he had said I knew there was no way to rectify the situation. Kevin was history.

After work that night I went to Kevin's house as I felt he could probably use a friend to talk to. When I got to his house I knocked on the door. Kevin opened it and without saying a word he motioned me in. When I got inside and looked at his face, his eyes were red and teary. I said, "What's up buddy?" As he started to speak he broke into sobs.

His bad day didn't end with running out of gas, getting a ticket and losing his job. When he arrived at his house his wife asked why he was home so early. He said he blew up at her and started swearing and throwing things. The more she was trying to find out what was wrong the madder he got until finally he told her to get the hell out, and she did. As she walked out of the door she said she wanted a divorce.

Then Kevin totally broke down in tears and said, "How could I do that? I love her so much."

I didn't think that this would be a good time to offer any advice. I thought the best thing I could do was to listen, and I did so for a couple of hours. I definitely didn't think it would be a good time to give Kevin the torn ticket that was in my pocket.

This story does have a happy ending. Kevin found a new job a week later at the Volkswagen dealership in town. His wife came back to him and they ended up having two children and pretty solid marriage that has survived to this day.

Kevin is just one example of something I have witnessed in my life when people let a molehill problem escalate into a mountain of grief. In this case it cost him his job and almost his wife.

Lord knows that I have been guilty of doing the same thing. What I've come to understand is that this happens because we feed the dragon by staying focused on a temporary unpleasant event instead of wiping it off and moving on.

Kevin's first mistake was putting off getting gas for his car. In the morning he paid the price for his blunder. But that should have been the end of it. By the afternoon he was back on the road and the problem was solved. He should have learned a lesson and moved on. Instead, he made a second and more critical mistake by staying focused on his past miscue and ended up paying a much higher price than he did for his first error.

When the dragon's breathing, it's hard to remain calm. The trick is to concentrate on the solution and then he will remain asleep. By doing so you are learning how to be a dragon tamer.

They are your inner feelings, owned by you, not the outside world. Mastering your own thoughts is the key to keep the dragon's fire from burning you from the inside out.

We must learn to accept a bummer for what it is. It is either something that we can resolve and put our energy into resolving. Or we can realize that there is no solution, bury it in the past, realizing that soon enough it will be a cartoon we didn't get to finish, and move on. The only other alternative I can think of is to dance with the dragon. Ouch, that really hurts.

Most bummers that can be fixed will just need you to do two things. First, come up with a game plan that will solve it. Second, follow the plan.

I wish there was an answer that would make all of the hassles in life disappear. The truth is they will be solved and forgotten by the time the Bus arrives; preferably much sooner. But for now, we are at the Bus Stop and there isn't a simple answer to make them magically vanish. But you can follow the game plan you outlined to resolve them.

Once you learn how to remain at peace on the inside regardless of outside circumstances you have the tackled the problem. Once you have tackled the problems why would you ever punch a hole in the wall or get so upset that you say and do things that you really didn't mean?

A lot of things get out of control because we let them. You have a small task, but you elected to put it off. If you don't take care of the daily minor details and let them accumulate, they will become overwhelming.

If you don't rinse off the dirty dishes and place them in the dishwasher, you will end up leaving them in the sink or worse on the table or counter. Two or three meals later the couple of dishes become a pile of dishes. Five meals later you get overwhelmed by the huge stack of dishes and dirty counters. Now the dragon is breathing, causing a state of depression because of the mess that you created. Ouch that hurts.

What was once an easy task of rinsing off a few plates is now a much tougher job. You now have to deal with a lot of encrusted dishes because of the leftover food that is caked on them. If only you'd taken a second or two to do the right thing, and simply rinse them off and put them in the dishwasher.

Many times the dishes don't get put in the dishwasher because it was already full of clean dishes. Bummer! Take a minute and unload it, or wait for the day when the dishes pile up, and feel the pain because now you have a much more difficult task to accomplish. (I hope that you understand that the dishes represent many things in life that come our way.)

The trick is to stay in motion handling small, lightweight chores and responsibilities. When there is enough laundry to do a load then do it. Don't wait until it piles up. When the yard needs mowing, do it now. Don't wait until it's a major hassle, making it much harder to mow. Either way it needs to get done. One way is easy, the other way it hurts.

I have used household chores as my example to the many other things we need to do or solve in our lives. Life is filled with responsibilities. When you put them off, all they do is pile up. When this happens it normally affects your attitude and you can become very unpleasant to be around. Your attitude not only affects you, but it also affects the people you care most about.

In my experience, life is pretty much made up of two things. There are things we *want* to do and things we *need* to do. The things we want to do are normally fun, entertaining or goal accomplishing. Things like writing your book, going fishing, bowling or hanging out with friends and family. Maybe it's something as simple as watching a movie or flying a kite.

Many times we don't do or enjoy the things we want to do, because we feel buried by the things we need to do. The reason we are buried is that we let the little things pile up.

Before I learned how to tame my own dragon, I had a hard time doing the things I enjoyed most in life. I was too busy being depressed over all the things I had to do. Because I was depressed, I was in the wrong state of mind to take care of them, so I routinely put them off. Because I did, I created an ever increasing backlog of things to do and then I became even more depressed. It was an endless circle.

I learned a simple thing that has helped me tremendously when it comes to getting things done. Before I go to bed at night I make a list of things that I want to accomplish tomorrow. By having a list I have created a map to get to where I want to go. The next step is to put myself in motion working toward crossing something off the list.

I don't worry about the entire list. I just concentrate on the first one. I do them one at a time, crossing them off until I have a blank piece of paper or a clear mind.

I know there are only so many hours in the day. I suggest that when you make the list you decide how much time you want to devote to each chore. If the list is especially long, you should also include sometime for yourself. Plan something that you want to do.

I also know that there are days when the things you need to do will consume most of the day. We all have days like that and we cannot predict them. The good news is that if you are in motion doing your chores, you will end up with less responsibilities to do tomorrow, leaving you more time to do the things you want to do.

But most days are not like that. Many of the things you need to accomplish are as simple as rinsing off the dishes. You just need to put yourself in motion taking care of them, so they don't pile up. You are the writer of your list. You are the director of how to get everything done. You are the actor who is following the script. If your personal movie is a dud and you choose to not write the script or act it out, you will end up with a harder, longer list of things to do tomorrow.

Most of us wake up in the morning with dragon breath. That's okay because there's toothpaste and mouth wash to fix that problem. What you don't want is to wake up feeling the dragon burning inside of you because you created a longer list of things to do today. Ouch, that hurts.

By having this kind of Bus Stop attitude, and working your list, you will not create the inner feeling of depression and despair. Now it will not hurt as much if at all.

If you have been letting the dragon burn in you and causing negative reactions while dealing with the hassles of life, it's okay because that was then and this is now. The past is a great place to make that mistake. But as far as today and your future goes, you can choose to not have to say, "Ouch that hurts!"

The first step is to believe that you have that choice and that you are the one who chooses. You are the king or queen of your inner thoughts and of your actions. So be a good leader. Write your list and lead yourself to inner contentment while waiting for your Bus at the Bus Stop.

Another self-inflicted wound is arguments. I have watched too many of them spin out of control. Most arguments are with someone you care about. Sometimes the argument is with children. Sometimes the adult acts like a child.

I once witnessed a couple throwing things at each other and exchanging some pretty rotten words they'd surely regret. Are you ready for this? They were arguing over which kind of tuna fish tasted better. How stupid. Everybody is entitled to their own opinions. Every person is living their own Bus Stop. Their ideas, tastes and opinions will many times be different from yours. This should be very easy to understand and accept, yet often it is not.

Several years ago I watched two salesman lose their job because neither one of them was willing to back down from their point of views. Chris and Dave, who were not the best of friends, were constantly chirping at each other. Apparently they had each talked to the same customer on two different days.

Our procedure was that whenever you finished talking to a customer the next step was to enter the customer's information onto a log sheet. If you did this and the customer came back and bought a car from a different salesman you got half of the commission. You also got half the commission if the client asked for you but for one reason or another you were not available to talk to him.

Chris had talked to someone the day before but failed to enter him into the log sheet. The next day the customer came back and did not ask to speak to Chris when Dave greeted him.

I could tell that Chris was fuming as he paced back and forth muttering while watching Dave and the customer talk. I asked him what was wrong. He told me that Dave knew that he had talked to the customer yesterday and was convinced the customer asked for him but Dave did not turn the prospect over to Chris.

The customer took a test ride and then left after Dave gave him his business card. Then Dave came inside to enter the client's information. Chris exploded in anger.

Dave acknowledged with a smirk that he saw Chris with the prospect yesterday but the customer did not ask for him so he took the Up. (An "Up" is car salesman slang for customer.) Dave wanted to apply the rule of losing out if you did not log the customer. Chris yelled out, "There is no way he wouldn't have asked for me!" The argument started to heat up.

Mr. Bloomer heard the commotion and stepped in as any sales manager would. He told them to both back down or they would lose their jobs. He then said he would call the customer after lunch and get the scoop.

As salesman we were never allowed to call a customer to see if he had asked for us because it could cause uncomfortable feelings. But Mr. Bloomer was a smooth, genuine and sincere talker and really knew how to put someone at ease.

But before he could make the call the whole situation blew up. The next thing you knew, Chris and Dave were outside in the parking lot in a full-fledged fist fight. Mr. Bloomer was a stocky man. He came running out and positioned himself between the two salesmen giving them each a push backwards. He kinda danced around holding out his arms talking to them until finally they both calmed down. Mr. Bloomer took both salesmen into his office. The end result was that they both got fired.

Mr. Bloomer told the rest of the salesmen not to go home after work as we were going to have a meeting. When we were all gathered together that night he said he never wanted to see such idiotic behavior again. He continued by saying that he hoped it was obvious that if there was this kind of behavior you would lose your job.

Then Mr. Bloomer said, "I did all I could do to try and settle Chris and Dave down. I didn't want them to lose their jobs, but they kept spouting off. Finally, I told them to take a week off and calm down and think about it. They both thought that I was being unfair and said some pretty rude things to me, so I let them both go. After they left I called the customer out of curiosity to get his side of the story. He said he did not ask for Chris; he didn't know it was important to do so. Obviously Chris did not build a good personal relationship with his customer or he would have asked for him."

Mr. Bloomer had told us this many times but he reiterated it again. He said that many customers don't understand commissions, and it was our job to build a friendly relationship with them so they would naturally ask to speak to their new friend.

"You see," Mr. Bloomer explained. "Dave knew the customer was talking to Chris yesterday, but he did a greedy thing and didn't turn him over to him. Chis knew he was supposed to log his customer but failed to do so. If either one of them did the right thing, there would have not been a problem. Even so, if just one of them had backed down they would still be working here; but they elected to fight it out with themselves and me. Now they are both looking for a new job.

The punch line is when Mr. Bloomer talked to the customer he told him that he decided not to buy a car from us and had already made a deal elsewhere. So Chris and Dave fought each other and lost their jobs for nothing."

The rest of the salesmen were not happy about saying goodbye to Chris and Dave. They were nice guys and we all liked them. Both of them had said more than once that of all the dealerships where they had ever worked, ours was their favorite. But unfortunately they chirped their way out of a good job. They didn't understand that Mr. Bloomer was trying to help them but instead they felt he was dumping on them. Over the years I have seen many uncomfortable situations and arguments over a minor detail. All it took was for someone to back down and let it go. Many times those involved were offered good advice on how to overcome what was bothering them but they ignored it, feeling the information directed at them was not in their best interest.

Too often they were angry and beyond caring. Ultimately, they ended up losing the battle because they did not heed the advice or change their attitude.

When I heard the following cute story it reminded me of the Chris and Dave's drama and many other situations I have witnessed in my life. I wish I could say that I never made the mistake that the Chirping Bird made but I have. I just do my best to not do it anymore.

The Chirping Bird

One day a bird determined he was the smartest bird in the world. The reason he felt this way was because he had decided not to fly south for the winter. He reasoned that it didn't make any sense to fly all the way there, just to turn around, and fly all the way back. Yep, this bird thought he was smarter than nature.

None of the other birds knew why they were flying south either, but they decided to go with the flow, and follow nature's path. They bid their friend farewell and began their journey.

"Suckers," the bird who stayed behind thought as he watched them fly away in a southerly direction. He was positive they would say he was the smartest bird of all when they returned.

Well, as time passes, the weather changed, and it began to get real cold. The bird had never stuck around before to experience what cold was like. "Oh, I get it," the bird said. "This is why we fly south for the winter. Winter means cold. I guess I'm not so smart after all," he concluded.

The bird began flying south for the winter to escape the cold, but he had waited too long. The ground was frozen, so he couldn't eat. Then ice began to form on his wings, and he knew he wasn't going to make it.

"That's it," the bird said out loud. "I just can't go on. I thought that I was the smartest bird in the world, but it turned out that I was the dumbest. I'm not going to cry about it though. I live by my decisions, but now I will die by one."

The bird gave one last flap of his wings then tucked them in. He began spinning down to earth and landed in a cow pasture. He lay there quietly quivering and waiting to die.

An old milk cow witnessed the bird's fall from the heavens and decided to go check it out. The cow sniffed the bird a few times then quickly lost interest. He turned his back to the bird and began grazing. Without giving it a second thought, the cow did what cows do and took a dump, which just so happened to completely cover the bird.

Realizing what just happened, the bird asked, "Why? Why did this have to happen to me? I was willing to take responsibility for my decision. I wasn't crying about it. I was taking it like a real bird. So why is it that the last thing that life is going to do is dump all over me? That's really cold!" Then, "Wait a minute, this stuff isn't cold. It's really warm."

In a short time the ice melted off of him and he completely warmed up. Shortly thereafter worms started popping up out of the ground, drawn to the warmth. The bird saw this and said, "Great! Lunch time!" Then he began eating until he was stuffed.

"You know what," the bird said to himself. "I *am* the smartest bird in the world. I'll get out of the cold by going from cow pasture to cow pasture."

Well, the bird began doing what most birds would do when they feel full of themselves, he began chirping away. Unfortunately, there was a cat in the pasture who heard the cow pile chirping. The cat had seen many things while living on the farm, but he'd never heard a cow pile chirp. You know how curious cats are, so he went to check it out.

When the cat got to the chirping cow pile, he began slapping at it to see where the sound came from. He did this until he uncovered the bird. "Great! Lunch!," the cat thought, then he ate the bird -- End of story.

There are three important lessons to be learned from this story:

First: Not everyone who dumps on you is necessarily your enemy.

Second: Not everyone who helps get you out of a mess is necessarily your friend.

Finally, and most importantly, if you are happy enough in a crappy situation keep your mouth shut.

The first lesson really applies to children, but there are children in us all, no matter what our age. Parents seem to be unfair, from a child's point of view, when they are not allowed to do whatever they want. They think that they are being dumped on when they are told no or told to clean their room or do the dishes.

Children need to be guided and taught to have a responsible and a safe life. But at the time you are trying to teach them, they feel dumped on. They don't understand that what you ask will be just another cartoon they didn't get to finish. The problem with children is they still believe the cartoon is a top priority.

Many times in life, people will try to offer advice with the best intentions of helping out, but we feel as if they are dumping on us. There have been times in my life that after I thought about what they said, it made sense and helped me have a better time at the Bus Stop.

Never be afraid to listen to others. Maybe you'll take their advice on the spot. Maybe you won't but after giving it some thought, you do. Or maybe you gave it some consideration and elected to pass on the advice. Sometimes words hurt, but later you find you needed to hear them and they weren't dumping on you after all.

Mr. Bloomer tried his hardest to help settle the problem between Chris and Dave. Unfortunately, they were both caught up in the frustration of trying to prove their point of view and chirped away. They had an uncontrollable desire to hear that they were right. They also felt that our sales manager was dumping on them by having them take a week off. So instead of backing off and taking the time for it to become another unwatched cartoon, they became unemployed.

The second lesson concerns the list of responsibilities you have made for yourself. Hopefully you have a short, easy list because you've been cleaning up small messes so they haven't piled up on you. Why does the list grow longer and harder? It's simple. Once you made the list you decided to stop being in motion by taking care of them.

I understand that there are times when we must put the list down and deal with other situations. I'm not talking about that. I am saying many people do what children do. They put off doing the list because something else sounded like more fun. They thought it would take them out of the situation they were in. But really it will only make the pile higher for them tomorrow and it will stink all the more because tomorrow has its own list of things to get done.

Once you are in motion taking care of your list, many times obstacles will appear trying to get us to put the list away. Friends offer to do something or go somewhere.

There are times you will have to say, "Thanks, but no thanks. I have other things to do." Or it could be your own inner voice trying to talk you into watching a movie which can easily turn into two movies with a nap in between. Now the day is gone and tomorrow's list is twice as long.

Don't get me wrong. I like to go places. I like to have fun. I love a nap. But we are not children anymore, we have responsibilities and they won't go away. They will just pile up. Then what? You guessed it. Ouch, that hurts.

So it comes down to this: Take care of the list first, then do the things you want to do. Be a master of your time. Be the parent of your inner childhood and get your chores done so they don't consume you.

As far as the third lesson goes, more than once I have chirped my way out of a good situation. It was just that I got caught up in the moment's frustration and said and did things I didn't mean.

I have witnessed employees who chirped about the 2% of their job that they didn't like, instead of thinking about the 98% they did like. Next thing they knew, they were out looking for a job.

I'm sure you can come up with some chirps you have seen, and maybe you've done it yourself, turning a good situation into something bad. That's okay if you did, because it's in the past. Apologize and/or rectify it if you can. Just do your best not to do it again.

I want to bring up arguments again. Many arguments are based on a point of view that is different from ours. If the discussion starts to become an argument that is getting out of control, I suggest you say the words, "You're right, I see where you are coming from." It very hard to argue with someone who agrees with you. These simple words can end most pending arguments with a hug, kiss or a handshake.

This is much better than the alternative. At the time you might be thinking that they are an idiot but nobody knows what you are thinking unless you tell them. It will soon become just another cartoon you didn't get to finish stacked with the others that are in your past. Who cares about them? I for one never spend anytime feeling mad or bad about an argument I used to have.

You might consider the possibility that you are wrong. More than once I thought I was so right to only later discover that I was wrong. It happens a lot in life, doesn't it?

Another thing is to stay true to your word. Be careful what you say and choose your words wisely. When we say we are going to do something that someone else is depending upon and then we don't do it, it is easy to understand that they feel let down. Now you may have put them in touch with the dragon and now they hurt.

One of the favorite lines I ever heard was in the movie *The Freshman*. In it Marlon Brando says something to Matthew Broderick. Matthew replies with, "Do you Promise?" Marlon answers by saying, "Everything I say, by definition, is a promise."

I know that sometimes we can have the greatest intentions, yet we're not able to do what we say. When this happens, offer a very sincere apology and do your best to make it right.

There is an old saying that goes: Say what you mean and mean what you say. It is a great philosophy. I love it because except for circumstances beyond our control, only we can break our word. If we stay true to what we say we will have far less bummers for ourselves as well as others.

When I was twelve years old my dad made a promise to me that he did not keep. I hid my sorrow deep inside and did not reveal my disappointment. I cherish the memory of it today.

Lemco and the Lemons

To this day I believe I started a new trend. It was 10 years before air bands became a craze but 1966 in 6th grade I had formed a group called *Lemco and the Lemons*. There were four of us in the band. At recess we were allowed to go into a vacant room and work out our routine. We would play an album by the group *Herman's Hermits*. While the music was playing I would lip sing the words as the other members played 'instruments'. The guitars were broom handles; the drums were empty oatmeal containers.

We became pretty popular with our peers. Many of the kids, instead of playing outside during recess, came into our room to watch our show. It became standing room only and was backed up to the hallway.

Our teacher came to check us out one day and was pretty impressed. She was impressed enough to book our next seven gigs. She arranged for us to play for every class in our school. To top it off, our grand finale was to be a live performance for the Bonney Lake PTA. Wow, we really felt as if we'd made the big time.

My mom and dad promised that they would go to the meeting to watch me perform. I was looking forward to having them in the audience. When the time came for us to start, I got some sad news. My dad's friend, Chuck, had called him and said his car was broken down and asked my dad if he could bring him jumper cables. My dad agreed and told me he should be able to make it back in time to watch me and the other guys do our show. I got an empty feeling in my stomach.

Our group went all out for the big day. We wore black turtle necks under our white shirts, black pants and Beatle shoes. While we were pantomiming the three songs you could see how much the audience liked us. They were taking pictures, clapping their hands to the rhythm, smiling and gave us a long round of applause when we finished.

While we were taking our bows my eyes scanned the parents. There was my mom, but no dad. I had hoped that he might make it before we finished but that was not to be. I must admit that did not stop me from soaking in the applause and noticing the smile on my mom's face but I also felt let down.

Not long after I got home my dad arrived. He asked me how it went. Before I could answer, my mom said; "It was so cute." She used words like awesome, fantastic and entertaining. She then told dad that he blew it and should have been there.

My dad looked pretty sad when he said to me, "I know I should have been there kid. It was a once in a life time opportunity and I should have gone. I could have told Chuck I had plans. I'm sure he could have called someone else. I would have been there in time but the jumper cables didn't solve the problem so I had to give him a ride home. I'm so sorry son."

I did feel let down but I told him it was okay and not to worry about it, but he did. For months he would bring it up every now and then and say, how sorry he was that he missed my performance. I could tell he was hurt a lot more than I was by his broken promise. I was well over it but he wasn't.

That summer on my dad's birthday my mom talked him into going for a walk. When they got back she blindfolded him and delivered him to the living room. Then the music started. My mom removed the blindfold and there we were. The four original members of Lemco and the Lemons were rearing to go. We went all the way. We wore our black turtle necks, white shirts and Beatle shoes with brooms sticks in hand

and oatmeal drums to pretend to play. Instead of doing the three songs we did at the PTA we air banded the entire album.

At first my dad was shocked and a bit teary eyed, but soon he was all smiles and was dancing in place. He even knew some of the words to the song *Mrs. Brown You Have a Lovely Daughter* and sang them with us. When we finished he asked us all to give him autographs. He kept that piece of paper on his wall until the day he died. I still have it.

The promise broken by my father should never have been broken, but my dad realized it too late. For months he felt an internal sadness and disappointment in his decision. To tell the truth it hurt me more than I let on. But it was resolved and became one of my family's favorite memories.

My dad learned a lesson about keeping a promise, but I learned a bigger one. I saw how much my dad was hurt because he broke his word to me. I learned a promise works both ways. By letting someone down you hurt them. By letting someone down you also hurt yourself. Much better to do all you can to keep your promises and not make them lightly. Remember…your spoken words are promises.

How I wish all of the things I've been told or promised had come true. I understand that some disappointments couldn't be helped and they are easy to forgive. But many times I was told something with empty intentions. We can't control what others say. But we can be true to our own words. You are the captain of your words. Use them wisely so that you won't disappoint anyone, including yourself.

Chapter Thirteen
The Gift of Time

A Precious Gift that we are all born with is the time that we are allotted in our life. It will come, and it will go. What you do with it and the attitude you have while doing it will determine the quality of your existence at the Bus Stop.

Have you ever noticed how water going down a drain spins? The outside takes longer to go around than the inside. The closer it comes to the end the faster it spins. I feel life goes by like that.

When I was younger, I felt the school day lasted forever. When my children went to school, it seemed like they were back home an hour after they left. As a parent it was only yesterday that my adult children were babies. Realizing this helps me to cherish my time.

Many people spend their lives striving to gain money and possessions. But what good are they if you are unhappy and not enjoying the day? Many a millionaire and famous people have arranged to meet their bus ahead of schedule. They discovered that what they had obtained still left them feeling empty and in despair.

Don't get me wrong. It is perfectly normal to want to have nice things for you and your loved ones. You should have goals and dreams and a *zest for the quest* to fulfill them. I am not trying to slow you down from obtaining them. I am suggesting that you have a game plan that allows you the time to enjoy the things that are free to own. Many of them are priceless.

I have goals and dreams. If this book sells a million copies, I'll have captured one of them. I'll also buy a few nice things for myself and others; but if it doesn't do well at the book stores, well, I had a great time writing it. Either way I win.

My father told me something on his death bed that I never will forget. He said, "Son, don't spend your time worrying about the things you don't have, because when the end comes, you'd trade all of your things for the time that you always had. Always appreciate the moment."

It took many years for that message to sink in. Then one day I realized how smart I was as a kid. How easy it was to be happy. I grew up about as poor as anyone, yet I had a childhood that even I envy. I didn't know it then, but I was experiencing the best life had to offer. I was in tune with the precious gift of time.

Right after I graduated from high school I married my ninth grade girlfriend, Cindy, and moved to Albany, Oregon. I went to work for my oldest brother, Ed.

As I've already mentioned he owned a small Suzuki motorcycle dealership. In a few short years it had expanded to Honda motorcycles and Honda cars. At the age of 22, I was promoted to general sales manager. I had a new house, cars, and lots of other nice things. The problem was, the nice things came with monthly payments.

As a result I was working about seventy hours a week. I had to. How else could I make the money to pay for the nice things? The problem with that was I was too tired to enjoy my nice things when I got home; the main one being my wife.

For the first time in my life I had valuable possessions. For the first time in my life I was stressed out and exhausted. For the first time in my life I got divorced. For the first time in my life I was having no fun.

I finally came to the conclusion that possessions can possess. I began to realize who owned whom. What I had been doing was exchanging the most valuable possession I owned, my time, to the banks and finance companies in order to possess the things that I didn't have the time to enjoy. (Kind of a Zen riddle isn't it.)

Somewhere along the way, I'd begun to believe that it was all about my job and possessions. I started believing that it was those things that determined who you are, that they were the way you measured success. As a result I'd lost the child that had always been in me. Fun was replaced by work; joy was replaced by stress. I went from being free to becoming owned by the lenders. I had little or no time for fun, friends, or family, certainly no time for my wife.

Finally, I came to realize that time is the greatest gift. It is my most prized possession. I will never again trade it unreasonably. We must all pay the rent and other necessities. We have all got to eat; that's a fact of life. But after we have covered those obligations, what we do with the rest of our time is strictly up to us.

You can spend all of your time trying to get more things if that's what you want. It's your Bus Stop. Or you can save some of your quality time doing things that have great rewards. "Where is the money going to come from for you to do fun things," you ask? Well, I wrote the following poem in hopes it would answer that question.

How much does it cost, to dig up worms, and go fishing?
How much does it cost, to play catch with your son?
How much does it cost, to have a conversation?
How much does it cost to have fun?
How much does it cost to read a book?
How much does it cost to kiss your wife?
How much does it cost to hug your children?
How much does it cost to enjoy life?
How much does it cost to reason?
How much does it cost to see?
How much does it cost to understand?
The best things in life are free.

If you lose your focus about all of the wonderful things you have and the things you can do, you might end up searching for what you already have, and that is the precious gift of time. The problem is all the money in the world can't buy back the time gone by.

All material things can do is make you feel like you are having a better time at the Bus Stop. Tell me, how many of those things are you planning to take with you? That's right you've got to leave them all behind. Nobody really owns anything. All you can do is rent them for a short while.

What I hope for you and your quest for material things is that when you get back on the Bus that you feel it was worth what it took to obtain them. That you feel it was a fair exchange of your time. If you do, then it was worth the investment. Otherwise, I think you need a different game plan.

My brother Ed sadly passed away in July of 2011. He died a wealthy man. He owned a big house in St. Croix in the Virgin Islands. He had his own yacht and airplane. He deserved to have them. He worked very hard and long to get them.

I have never known anyone who worked as much as he did. The beauty of it is, he loved working. Because of his inner drive to succeed at what he loves to do, he had become a self-made millionaire and owned plenty of nice things as a consequence. I understand why my brother did what he did, and I am extremely proud of him.

I once described his perfect day to him. I said that after working all day your wife brought dinner to your office. She then made love with you there. That way you wouldn't have to go home and you could stay and work all night. He smiled then said, "Yep. That would be a perfect day."

There is no doubt in my mind that Ed got his time's worth. It didn't matter to me if he made a lot of money or not, just as long as he enjoyed the wait at the Bus Stop. And he really did. It was not the things he enjoyed the most; he was not home long enough to spend time with them. But he did love the time spent earning them.

On the other side of the coin, Ed did not quite understand why I live as I do. He knew that I took a lot of time off and hung out with my friends and family. He also knows that I did not have many nice things.

Ed sold his dealerships and started his own motorcycle consultant company called Ed Lemco and Associates. He also was the CEO of one of the largest motorcycle chains in the UK. One day he had me fly to England do some sales training for his sales staff.

After one of my training seminars, Ed and his wife took me out to a nice dinner. They had just bought a new Jaguar and were pretty excited about it.

I said, "Yeah, it must be nice."

Ed looked over at me, and with a bit of disappointment said, "You know, you could have a car like this if you would just work more often." I replied that I was happy with what I was driving.

He said, "I don't see how. I've seen your car. It's seven years old with almost a hundred thousand miles on it."

I answered that it was a good running car and more important than that, it was paid for. I explained to him that it got me home from the places it took me, and that's what really counted.

To me, a car is mostly the top half of the steering wheel, the windshield, the radio and the heater knobs. That's what I see about 95% of the time, and they all worked just fine. I figure the rest of the car is meant to make us feel good about ourselves. It's nice to get compliments about our things. It makes a lot of people feel good. The problem with that theory is, I already feel good.

Ed still didn't understand, so I tried to explain it this way. "You see Ed. If I had a car as nice as yours, I wouldn't park it in the street. I would park it in the garage." Ed agreed that would be the smart thing to do.

"It's like this," I continued. "I don't have a garage. So I'd have to get a different house with a garage just so my car could sleep inside. The car I have now never complains about staying outside." Ed just shook his head over my rationality.

"Look," I said sincerely, "besides having to come up with a big cash down payment, I would also end up with pretty high car payments for years to come. My insurance would go way up along with my rent because now I have to pay for the garage. In order to afford all of this I would have to spend months of my time working far away from the things I love, just to end up with a car that will take me places like the one I have now does. The main difference would be I would have all of those added expenses. The highest one would be my time."

Of course, Ed didn't agree. But I understood why. Ed's work was his love. So when he was working, he is also enjoying his time waiting for his Bus, just as I am. The big difference is, Ed got to rent nicer things than I do.

Time is my gold and I do my best to protect it. I enjoy visiting with my family and friends a lot more than I would be driving around in a Jaguar if it meant I had to give them up. Sure, I would like to have both, but I won't sacrifice the one to only have the other.

There are two main points I'm trying to stress. The first is to make sure that it is worth the time to obtain that which you desire. You should also consider what effect that will have on your loved ones. The time spent pursuing the gravy for your potatoes could cause you to end up with a cold plate of potatoes. Or you might discover that someone else has already eaten them.

I have seen it more than once that someone focused too hard to get what they wanted but didn't take the time to appreciate what they already had. Then, once they possessed what they were after, they discovered what they once had was no longer there; be it things, people, feelings or time. The worst part came when they realized that what they once had was worth far more than what they were trying to gain or had gained.

The second point I'd like to make is that waiting at the Bus Stop can be a wonderful experience, no matter who you are or what you have. If you are waiting to enjoy your day until you have everything you want, you are being possessed by the things you don't even have. If you turn that focus inward and appreciate what is all around you, you just might discover you already own what it is you are seeking for.

When my son and daughter were old enough to learn one of the secrets of life, I taught it to them with a song. Sometimes when they wanted something, I got it for them. Other times when they asked, I began singing versus from one of the hits from the Rolling Stones. The lyrics went as followed; "*You can't always get what you want. No, you can't always get what you want. But if you try sometime, you just might find. You get what you need."*

When I started singing that song my children would start begging and say, "No Daddy, don't sing that song again!" Then we would normally start laughing and soon they forgot what it was they wanted.

I wasn't always able to get the things my children wanted. Sometimes I wished I could afford them, but I wasn't in the position to do so. Oh, well. They had me to sing to them. I could take them to the park or the lake. I could play with them or read them a story. I gave them the greatest gift a parent can give their children and that was my love and my time.

The Old Woman

A woman once came out of her house and saw three old men with long white beards sitting in her front yard talking to each other. She did not recognize them. She said, "I don't think I know you, but if you are hungry. Please come in and have something to eat."

"Is your husband home?" they asked.

"No," she said. "He's out. He will not be home until after he gets off work."

"Then we cannot come in," they replied.

In the evening when her husband came home, she told him what had happened. He said, "Go tell them I am home and invite them in to eat dinner with us."

The woman went out and invited the men in. "We do not go into a house together," they said. One of the old men then explained. "His name is Wealth," he said pointing to one of his friends, and said pointing to another one, "He is Success, and I am Love." Then he added, "Now go in and discuss with your husband which one of us you want in your home."

The woman went in and told her husband who became very excited. "How nice," he said. "Since we have a choice, let us invite Wealth. Let him come and fill our home with wealth!"

His wife disagreed. "My dear, why don't we invite Success?"

Their young daughter was listening from the other corner of the house. She jumped in with her own suggestion: "Would it not be better to invite Love? Think how wonderful it will be if our house was filled with love!"

"Let us take our daughter's advice," said the husband to his wife. "Go out and invite Love to be our guest."

The woman went out and said to the three old men, "We want Love to come in and join us. Please come in and be our guest for dinner."

Love walked toward the house. The other two also got up and followed him. Surprised, the lady asked Love, "I thought I could only invite one of you, so I invited you. Why do the other two follow?"

The old men replied, "If you had invited Wealth or Success, the other two of us would've stayed outside; but since you invited Love, wherever I go, the other two go with me. Wherever there is Love, there is also Wealth and Success."

I am sure you get the point, but consider this. We must give our time to earn the great gift of love. It is one of the best exchanges life has to offer. I firmly suggest that you allocate some of your quality time to obtain it and not let the pursuit of material things block its path.

The Gambler

There was a gambler whose wife needed an operation or she might die. So he went to his rich uncle and said, "Uncle, please loan me $20,000 for an operation for my wife or she might die."

The uncle pondered his suggestion with concern and then said. "Nephew, I know you are a gambler. How do I know you will spend the $20,000 on the operation and not gamble it away?"

"Oh, you don't have to worry about that uncle. You see, I have $20,000 put away for gambling. I just need another $20,000 for her operation."

The $20,000 represents time. I have witnessed several people who had the time to pursue their outside interests only to leave very little quality time for the ones that they love and the ones who love them. It's hard to stay emotionally close to someone if you don't invest the time to do it. Many good relationships have gone separate ways because someone did not give the time it takes to make it work. It is hard to stay in love if you are lonely.

What time you have left at your Bus Stop is yours to decide what to do with, and what to spend it on, and who to spend it with. There is no rich uncle to borrow time from. Your loved ones and friends may forget what you said, but they will never forget how you made them feel. To achieve those feelings will take an investment of your time. An investment that I believe is well worth it. When our time draws near to get back on the Bus, I believe it will be the love we gave and the love we received that will count as our greatest achievement.

You have today.
Maybe you will have tomorrow.
Use your time wisely.
And appreciate it for what it is.

Yesterday is history.
Tomorrow is a mystery.
Today is a gift.

That's why it's called the present!

Chapter Fourteen
Chasing a Dream

So Far I Have Discussed Bus Stops, attitudes, wise investment of time, dog crap, old owls and several other things. But how about you and the dreams you have? Are they important too? Of course they are, and you should do all you can to chase them. You just want to make sure that the chase is worth the time spent trying to achieve them.

I have a dream that my book will be a top seller. As I am writing it, I have no idea if anyone is going to read it. If you are reading it, then my dream is coming true. The point is that I *am* writing it. My dream is in motion. If it ends up just a manuscript in my computer, and my dream doesn't come true, then at the least, I lived the dream, and I had a blast doing it.

Whatever your dreams are, I hope you will pursue them if you believe the time spent is worth chasing them. Maybe you want to write a book or go on a great vacation. Maybe you want to build a house or take sky diving lessons. The list of dreams is endless. The important thing is that you have them. They can't come true if you don't.

Some of our dreams are waiting for the right time to chase them. I call them ' *dreams on the shelf*.' You might, for example, be waiting for the kids to graduate from high school. Your dream is to see them in college. It could be you are waiting to retire, and then take an extended vacation or move to a sun-belt state. Possibly you are looking forward to your next raise from work so you can buy something like a new car. There are hundreds of good reasons that put a dream on a shelf.

My definition of a dream on the shelf is that there is a plan to make it come true. You're just waiting for the right day to put the plan in motion. Without a plan you are only dreaming. Dreaming is okay; it's better than having no dreams at all, but it can't come true without a plan to make it so. The plan should be a step-by-step method of achieving your goal. A sophisticated rocket that goes to the moon was assembled one bolt, one step at a time. Try to see the whole picture then break it down into individual steps. Creating a road map to your destination is the surest way of arriving there.

Before I started writing this book I made a list of chapters. I then made notes concerning what each chapter would cover. I arranged them in order and then started writing, filling in the gaps. Bingo, I ended up with a book. The same procedure holds true to many other dreams that people are trying to fulfill.

In my experience many people didn't chase an affordable dream they had, that was worth their time pursuing because they were afraid it won't come true. They didn't chase it down because they were afraid of failure, to them I say, watch and learn from a baseball game.

When my Bus comes I would rather say that I struck out trying to get a hit, rather than saying I never came up to bat. The game takes players. It also requires people to sit in the stands watching. It's up to them to decide which one they want to be. Do they want to be a player or spectator? It's their call, their time and their dreams.

Whatever your dream might be, I believe the best way to capture it is to be passionate about the quest for it. Go after something you love to do. Enjoy working on the plan. The best way to get the job done is to make it fun. I love to write. But most of my earlier stuff never got printed. Still, I got to experience the joy of writing so I couldn't lose.

Throw in the fun and excitement of playing the game. This is something a lot of people don't realize. I get to live the dream. Dreaming is one of the cheapest entertaining things you can do. You should have lots of them.

If you go after one of your dreams and it doesn't work out, there might be several people saying to you, "I told you so." But when you have success those same people will say, "I knew you could do it." And then they will probably want to hop on your bandwagon.

There are two important things these people don't realize. They didn't understand that you were willing to risk striking out in order to get a hit. They didn't understand that you were also willing to risk failure in your quest for success. I truly believe that we only fail when we don't try to succeed.

The other thing is that you are a dream chaser, a player, and not a spectator. I will always believe it is a lot more fun to play a game then it is to watch it. Every game will end, even the spectator's game. There is no such thing as overtime. When the final out is made, we all have to get back on the Bus that brought us to the game. At the least you can say you took your swings. They get to say, "I was gonna."

I have chased many dreams in my lifetime that did not come true. I have chased others and had tremendous positive results. There is one that still amazes me.

When I was a teenager I was at a party when someone put on a record called: *The James Gang Rides Again*. I liked it a lot. The next day I went to the record store and bought it. I must have listened to it a hundred times over the following week. I loved the guitar work along with the lyrics and the voice of the lead singer. I studied the album cover and learned that a guy named Joe Walsh did all three. I thought about it for a while and then the goal was born.

One afternoon two good friends came over and I played the album for them. After it was over I said to them that one day I was going to meet Joe Walsh and we'll be friends. They looked at me as if I was crazy. One of them said, "Steve, you're such a big dreamer. The next thing you'll think is that you are going to join the band." Then they both started laughing at me. I don't think at the time they realized that calling me a dreamer was a compliment.

Over the next five years or so I did manage to meet Joe three times after his concerts. I would stand outside by the backstage door waiting for him to exit. When he did, he was glad to shake hands and sign autographs with his fans, but that was not my dream. Being a friend was the goal.

I eventually moved to Biloxi, Mississippi where I worked as sales trainer for my brother's consulting company. I had the southern region. One day while driving home from the airport, I read on the Coliseum marque that Joe Walsh was opening for Stevie Nicks. Personally, I thought it should have been the other way around.

I bought tickets and went home. While sitting on the couch I thought about my goal. I decided this was the right time to put it into motion. I wasn't exactly sure how I was going to pull it off. I did know that the first thing that would have to happen is that the two of us needed to meet again.

Biloxi is a coastal city off of the Gulf of Mexico. The main highway is lined with hotels. I figured Joe would be staying at one of the nicer ones close to the Coliseum. I waited until the day of the show, somewhere around noon and began driving down the highway, looking for limousines in the hotel parking lots.

I stopped at a red light beside the Hilton. Guess what cut right in front of me from the other direction and parked at the side of the building? Yep, it was Joe in a limo. I pulled up beside it and turned off my engine. As I stepped out of the car, Joe got out of the limo. "Hey Joe," I said. "How ya doin?"

Joe and I were in the parking lot uninterrupted. He gave me a good ten minutes of his time and then introduced me to Richard, his road manager. He asked Richard to arrange to have a couple of back stage passes for me. Richard said he would and that they would be waiting for me at the Will Call both. I thought, *How cool*.

When I got home, I was anxious to tell my wife what happened and that we were going back stage. Though I was excited about that, I still knew that my quest was far from over. I had met him again, but we were not friends.

That night I went to the Will Call ticket booth. Sure enough there was an envelope with my name on it, but it wasn't back stage passes, it was only tickets for the show but they were a lot better than the ones I had. We were now four rows back - dead center.

I stood there a few minutes, feeling a bit deprived, when I noticed Richard out front talking to some of the security people. I went up to him and asked if he had a minute. He said he did but to make it quick. I first thanked him for the tickets but then showed him the ones that I had already purchased.

"Richard," I said. "I thought it was back stage passes you were leaving."

Richard apologized and then said, "I'm so sorry but I've given away the passes I've been allotted. Can I buy you a drink tonight and make it up to you?"

I was saddened by the news, but I was more than happy to meet up with him and maybe figure out a way to talk some more with Joe.

After a great show, my wife and I went to the bar in the Hilton. Not long after, Richard showed up. We had a couple of drinks and talked. I told him I was a sales consultant and traveled all through the south.

Then Richard said how bad he felt about the passes and asked is there any way I could make it to the Memphis Tennessee show in two days. I thought about my schedule for a minute. I did have a client I needed to visit in Memphis, so I said I could make it.

He told me that for sure there would be back stage passes waiting for me at Will Call. He also said that he and the rest of the band would be staying at the Hyatt Regency and should arrive by three o'clock the day of the show.

Richard also mentioned in passing the travel names that the band used. He explained the reason the band had travel names was that if a fan tried to call a member of the band at the hotel, they wouldn't know who to ask for.

My wife was not able to go to Memphis, so I kissed her goodbye and took off. I had a lot of time to think and I hatched up a plan that I hoped would work. I got to the Hyatt around 11:00. I went up to the lady working the front desk and asked if any of the band members had checked in yet. Of course, I used their travel names.

She looked me over then said, "No, not yet. You must be with the band."

"Ta Da" I thought. The plan was working. I said, "Yes, I am. I must be the first one. The rest of the guys should be here soon." I then

145

gave her my name and she checked the band list. She looked concerned and then said, "I'm sorry but you are not on the list."

I smiled and said to check under my stage name and then made one up. She checked but frowned again and repeated that I was not on the list.

"Darn it," I said, shaking my head. I then said, "We hired a new girl in the Hollywood office and this is the second time she's done this to me." I smiled and said, "Not to worry. Just put the room on my personal credit card and I'll get reimbursed when I get back to the office."

She thanked me for understanding and then swiped my credit card. I then told her that I had some important information to go over with Joe. I didn't say Joe, of course. I used his road name. I asked that she put us in adjoining rooms, which she did.

When I got to my room, I unpacked my bag and then propped the door open. A little before 3:00 I heard the elevator open and people talking while walking toward my room. One of them was Joe. He stopped at my door and looked at me with bewilderment.

"Hey Joe, how ya doin?" I said, waving casually.

He took a few seconds to reply and then he asked me if this was my room? "Yes it is." I replied.

He then said, "Didn't I see you in Biloxi the other day?"

"That was me." I said as I smiled.

Joe pondered the situation a few seconds then asked if I had a ticket to the concert tonight. I told him I did. He said, "Good," then added that he would like to meet me in my room shortly after the end of the show because he wanted to talk to me about something.

I cheerfully replied, "Perfect. I want to talk to you about something too."

He shook my hand and asked my name again. I told him it was Steve. He said, "Okay Steve, I'll see ya later on tonight." My heart was beating fast and I was thinking, *Wow, Joe Walsh was at my door and is going to come over tonight for a visit. How cool is that.*

Right after the concert I made fast tracks to my room and waited anxiously for a knock on the door. About an hour later it happened.

When I opened the door there was Joe but he was not alone. He had a big, bad bodyguard by the name of Johnny D. with him. I invited them in. We all sat down around a round table in the room.

Joe looked at me and said, "Steve, when I got out of my limo in Biloxi, there you were. Then I come to Memphis and you not only get in my wing of the hotel, you get the room right next to me. When I book a hotel I block the wing, let alone the connecting room. You might be the nicest guy in the world or you might be another Mark David Chapman who shot John Lennon. I want to know how you did that."

I could easily understand his concern and felt the eyes of his bodyguard staring holes through me. I'd never given it a thought that he might think I was some kind of sick stacker. I told him the whole story from the beginning. Halfway through the story Joe began to laugh and feel comfortable about me. (You will have to read my book: <u>Joe & Me</u> to get the whole story.)

When I finished he said, "You know, we need someone like you working for us." He gave me a phone number to call and the name of Irving Azoff to ask for.

I never did follow up on his suggestion. I didn't think the rock and roll life was for me. I'd just become a first time dad and wanted to concentrate on the wonders of being a daddy. I just wanted to make friends with Joe.

Soon after I told Joe my story he told the bodyguard he could be on his way. Joe and I talked for over three hours that night. He told me some of his background. He talked about his brother's garage band and few other things about himself, but mostly we talked about more meaningful things like our children. He had a daughter named Lucy who was about the same age as my daughter Amy. We showed each other pictures of our kids and talked about the wonders of being a parent.

When it was time to call it a night, Joe said whenever I could make it to a performance I should look him up and say hi and he would get me backstage. He then said it was a true pleasure meeting me. I smiled. That was the vision I had told my two friends about.

I was very lucky that Joe is a cool guy. He could have got upset and had me thrown out of the hotel. But he didn't. He gave me some of his time and more importantly his friendship.

Over the last 25 years I have met up with Joe many times. He has always been so cool to me. Besides backstage passes he has come to a party I had and was great to my guests. He has had me sit on stage during a reunion show with the James Gang and even took my wife and me out to dinner with some of his family members.

No. Joe and I aren't best friends and that was not my goal. But I am confident if you go up to him and mention my name, he'll say that Steve Lemco is a friend of mine.

I had a dream and I chased it down. I was told I was crazy for having it. I was laughed at yet I made it come true. I ended up writing a book about it. It is my life story along with the adventures I had with Joe. It is called: *Joe & Me*. It is available at Amazon in paper back or Kindle.

(After the James Gang, Joe Walsh went on to have a very successful solo career. Today he is a member of the *Eagles*.)

Of course there are rules to chasing a dream because not every dream is achievable.

The Six Story Building

There was a woman who was walking down a city street. She noticed something she couldn't believe. There was a man standing on the sidewalk repeating to his self, "I know I can do it. I know I can do it." He would then run full blast, jump into the air, and crash into a six story building. Then he would pick himself up, wipe off the blood then repeat the process. Over and over he attacked the building with the same bloody results.

Finally, the woman just had to know why the man was doing it, so she went up and asked him.

"Lady," he said. "I bet a friend of mine that I could jump over the building."

The woman could not believe her ears and began to laugh.

"Mister," she said, "There is no way you will ever be able to jump over a six story building. What on earth has possessed you to try?"

"Simple," the man answered. "My friend gave me tremendous odds that I couldn't do it. When I jump over the building I'll be a rich man."

There are six story buildings in many people's lives. No matter how bad they want something it is just not obtainable. Before you begin a quest, you should anticipate the obstacles that might block your path. You want to make sure you can hurdle them.

I'm positive at my age that I cannot be the quarterback for the Seattle Seahawks although I would love to be. I can dream about it all I want but there is no way it will come true. It would be crazy for me to invest my time and or money trying to make it happen.

Besides ventures you want to take, things you'd like to obtain or places you'd like to visit, I'm also talking about the desire to have someone in your life that can't or won't be a part of your Bus Stop.

I've seen severely depressed people who weren't having any fun at their Bus Stop because they longed for another person. It could be a break up in a relationship, a divorce or sadly the loss of a loved one who's Bus has picked them up.

Yes, it is hard to have loved and lost. Letting go of someone who can't or won't be in your life can be one of the hardest emotional experiences to have.

If you have experienced it, but have now moved on, it meant you did one very important thing. More importantly, if you are going through it now and want to know what that important thing is in order to douse the dragon and move on, I will repeat it. *You feel what you think.*

Stinking thinking is the surest way to fuel the dragon. To control our thoughts is the major ingredient to inner contentment. If you remain focused on what you have lost, how can you feel anything but miserable?

Naturally, there should be a time for mourning when someone first finds out that someone they loved is no longer available to them. Sometimes it makes sense to take a time out from everyday responsibilities to rest and maybe cry. There is a season for everything. The seasons change, they move forward and so should we.

When my wife left me, I became absorbed with self-pity. All day long I would think about her and how much I wanted her back. Even though she remarried shortly after the divorce I still remained focused on what I lost. I went through a living hell trying to fix something that had no chance of being repaired.

I did the exact opposite of what I should have done. I stopped going to work. I put all of my friends on hold. I quit going places and doing things. I just sat around and focused on the one thing I didn't have instead of appreciating all of the blessing I still had. By doing that I gave the dragon free rein over my inner being and he burned me with a passion.

I spent years self-inflicting myself with negative thoughts. It was a full time endeavor. I was my own worst enemy. When the day came that I freed myself from my own web of depression, I realized how much sooner I should have and could have done it. I could have stopped the excruciating pain at the beginning of my ordeal.

Yes, I'd lost someone very dear to me and it made sense to feel sad for a while. But if I'd changed my thoughts from what I didn't have to the things and people I did have, I would have realized I had so much. If I'd stayed active in work, visiting with friends, doing things and going places, I would have cleared up the mess in my mind long before I did.

Misery is pretty much for loners. If ever you are going through it, the best thing I can say is think positive thoughts and stay active. Visit your family and friends. Go places and do things. Once I did that everything changed. Once I got active everything changed because I concentrated on what can be.

I will always believe that a positive attitude attracts good things as a negative one brings forth despair. I believe that with all of my heart because I have lived both sides of it.

The change in someone's attitude can only happen when they believe that they have control over what they focus on. Once they believe that and meditate on positive thinking, they will be motivated to move on from the grief of a loss.

There are times when we must let go. If all of your focus is on what you won't release and it is unattainable, you'll continue to crash into the six story building of life.

Sure, it's okay to have a season of mourning. That's only normal. But after you have done that for a while it is then time to walk around the building and feel the joy of living. Don't focus on what you have lost. Think of all you have and all that you can obtain. As the old story goes, when one door closes another one opens. I know that in my life there have been a lot of doors. Yes, there are many chapters in the book of life. I hope that the Bus driver tells you that your personal book of life was a best seller. I also hope that you have the best possible Bus Stop.

Thanks for reading my book

Special thanks to Roger Cooper for helping me with the editing. It was good seeing you ole buddy.

Other books by Steve Lemco available at Amazon.com

You Gotta-Wanna

Life at the Bus Stop

Joe & Me

Note:

My brother Ron wrote one of my favorite books that I have read. It's called: <u>Rest Stop</u>. It is a prison escape and pursuit novel. If you like Quentin Tarantino's style I am sure you will enjoy <u>Rest Stop</u>. It is available at <u>amazon.com</u> under Ron Lemco or by the title.

Steve Lemco Contact Information:

Phone: 253-826-6110 - PST

Email: stevelemco@aol.com

Reviews appreciated

Copies of this book are available at amazon.com or by emailing Steve. Please put Your Book in the header.

Made in the USA
San Bernardino, CA
13 July 2016